Nelson Thornes Framework English

Skills in Fiction

WESTMINSTER LIBRARIES

Geoff Reilly and **Wendy Wren**

Series Consultant: **John Jackman**

Contents

At 11 o'clock the family retired

When Mr Hiram B Otis, the American Minister, bought Canterville Chase, every one told him he was doing a very foolish thing, as there was no doubt at all that the place was haunted. However, the reactions of the American family to the old-English ghost are far from what might be expected!

At eleven o'clock the family retired, and by half past all the lights were out. Some time after, Mr Otis was awakened by a curious noise in the corridor, outside his room. It sounded like the clank of metal, and seemed to be coming nearer every moment. He got up at once, struck a match, and looked at the time. It was exactly one o'clock. He was quite calm, and felt his pulse, which was not at all feverish. The strange noise still continued, and with it he heard distinctly the sound of footsteps. He put on his slippers, took a small oblong phial out of his dressing-case, and opened the door. Right in front of him he saw, in the wan moonlight, an old man of terrible aspect. His eyes were as red burning coals; long grey hair fell over his shoulders in matted coils; his garments, which were of antique cut, were soiled and ragged, and from his wrists and ankles hung heavy manacles and rusty gyves.

'My dear sir,' said Mr Otis, 'I really must insist on your oiling those chains, and have brought you for that purpose a small bottle of the Tammany Rising Sun Lubricator. It is said to be completely efficacious upon one application, and there are several testimonials to that effect on the wrapper from some of our most eminent native divines. I shall leave it here for you by the bedroom candles, and will be happy to supply you with more should you require it.' With these words the United States Minister laid the bottle down on a marble table, and, closing his door, retired to rest.

For a moment the Canterville ghost stood quite motionless in natural indignation; then, dashing the bottle violently upon the polished floor, he fled down the corridor, uttering hollow groans, and emitting a ghastly green light. Just, however, as he reached the top of the great oak staircase, a door was flung open, two little white-robed figures appeared, and a large pillow whizzed past his head! There was evidently no time to be lost, so, hastily adopting the Fourth Dimension of Space as a means of escape, he vanished through the wainscoting, and the house became quite quiet.

On reaching a small secret chamber in the left wing, he leaned up against a moonbeam to recover his breath, and began to try and realise his position. Never, in a brilliant and uninterrupted career of three hundred years, had he been so grossly insulted. He thought of the Dowager Duchess, whom he had frightened into a fit as she stood before the glass in her lace and diamonds; of the four housemaids, who had gone off into hysterics when he merely grinned at them through the curtains of one of the spare bedrooms; of the rector of the parish, whose candle he had blown out as he was coming late one night from the library, and who had been under the care of Sir William Gull ever since, a perfect martyr to nervous disorders; and of old Madame de Tremouillac, who, having wakened up one morning early and seen a skeleton seated in an arm-chair by the fire reading her diary, had been confined to her bed for six weeks with an attack of brain fever, and, on her recovery, had become reconciled to the Church, and had broken off her connection with that notorious sceptic Monsieur de Voltaire. He remembered the terrible night when the wicked Lord Canterville was found choking in his dressing-room, with the knave of diamonds half-way down his throat, and confessed, just before he died, that he had cheated Charles James Fox out of £50,000 at Crockford's by means of that very card, and swore that the ghost had made him swallow it. All his great achievements came back to him again, from the butler who had shot himself in the pantry because he had seen a green hand tapping at the window pane, to the beautiful Lady Stutfield, who was always obliged to wear a black velvet band round her throat to hide the mark of five fingers burnt upon her white skin, and who drowned herself at last in the carp-pond at the end of the King's Walk. With the enthusiastic egotism of the true artist he went over his most celebrated performances, and smiled bitterly to himself as he recalled to mind his last appearance as 'Red Reuben, or the Strangled Babe', his début as 'Gaunt Gibeon, the Blood-sucker of Bexley Moor', and the furore he had excited one lovely June evening by merely playing ninepins with his own bones upon the lawn-tennis ground. And after all this, some wretched modern Americans were to come and offer him the Rising Sun Lubricator, and throw pillows at his head! It was quite unbearable. Besides, no ghost in history had ever been treated in this manner. Accordingly, he determined to have vengeance, and remained till daylight in an attitude of deep thought.

The next morning when the Otis family met at breakfast, they discussed the ghost at some length. The United States Minister was naturally a little annoyed to find that his present had not been accepted. 'I have no wish,' he said, 'to do the ghost any personal injury, and I must say that, considering the length of time he has been in the house, I don't think it is at all polite to throw pillows at him' – a very just remark, at which, I am sorry to say, the twins burst into shouts of laughter. 'Upon the other hand,' he continued, 'if he really declines to use the Rising Sun Lubricator, we shall have to take his chains from him. It would be quite impossible to sleep, with such a noise going on outside the bedrooms.'

For the rest of the week, however, they were undisturbed, the only thing that excited any attention being the continual renewal of the blood-stain on the library floor. This certainly was very strange, as the door was always locked at night by Mr Otis, and the windows kept closely barred. The chameleon-like colour, also, of the stain excited a good deal of comment. Some mornings it was a dull (almost Indian) red, then it would be vermilion, then a rich purple, and once when they came down for family prayers, according to the simple rites of the Free American Reformed Episcopalian Church, they found it a bright emerald-green. These kaleidoscopic changes naturally amused the party very much, and bets on the subject were freely made every evening. The only person who did not enter into the joke was little Virginia, who, for some unexplained reason, was always a good deal distressed at the sight of the blood-stain, and very nearly cried the morning it was emerald-green.

Oscar Wilde

TEXT LEVEL WORK

Comprehension

A 1 At what time was Mr Otis awakened?

2 Mr Otis suggested some oil that could help to reduce the noise.
What was the name of the oil?

3 The Canterville Ghost has happy memories of terrifying people over the centuries.
Name three of the people whom he haunted.

4 Mr Otis has several children but only one of them is named. What is this child's name?

5 For how many years had the ghost been haunting the Canterville home?

B 1 What is strange about the blood-stain on the library floor?

2 The ghost carries out his hauntings disguised as various characters.
Name two of his characters.

3 Who was responsible for throwing pillows at the ghost?

4 What do you think Oscar Wilde meant when he described the ghost as '*adopting the Fourth Dimension of Space*'?

5 Suggest reasons why Virginia '*was always a good deal distressed at the sight of the blood-stain, and very nearly cried the morning it was emerald-green*'.

C 1 What do you think of the American family described by Oscar Wilde in *The Canterville Ghost*?

2 In which ways is *The Canterville Ghost* a traditional ghost story and in which ways is it unusual for a ghost story?

3 Which features of the ghost's appearance do you think are traditionally associated with hauntings?

WORD LEVEL WORK

Vocabulary

Dictionary work

Use a dictionary and the context of the story to explain the meanings of the following words.

1 phial	4 manacles	7 efficacious	10 wainscoting
2 egotism	5 gyves	8 testimonials	11 martyr
3 furore	6 vermilion	9 kaleidoscopic	12 sceptic

Spelling

Root words and derivations

> We sometimes say that English words have their *roots* in other languages. So how did the English language develop?
>
> Before the Romans invaded Britain, the native peoples spoke Celtic dialects, related to Irish and Scottish Gaelic. The Romans, who occupied Britain from AD 43 to about AD 410, spoke a form of Latin and many of their words were absorbed into the local language.
>
> Modern English, as we speak it, actually begins to be recognisable from about 1500 and it is still changing and developing.
> Although Shakespeare can be difficult to understand, his writing is classed as Modern English.
>
> Many English words grew from Greek or Latin. You can often find the root Greek or Latin word inside an English word.

Copy the words from *The Canterville Ghost* in table 1 and match them with their Latin root words in table 2.

Table 1

insist	oblong	antique	efficacious	indignation	eminent
table	application	dimension	aspect	native	distinctly

Table 2

Latin root word	*Canterville Ghost* word
eminens	to be distinguished, prominent
nativus	birth
aspectus	countenance, face
efficacia	efficiency
distinctus	separate, distinct
insistere	to take a stand
dimensio	a measuring
tabula	a board, plank
antiquus	ancient, old
oblongus	rather long
indignans	to be angry, to be displeased
applicare	to join, to connect, to attach, to add

SENTENCE LEVEL WORK

Grammar and punctuation

Nouns and adjectives
Nouns

> Remember, a *noun* is a word that names something.
> There are different types of noun:
>   *common nouns*, eg match, eyes, bottle
>   *proper nouns*, eg Mr Otis, United States
>   *collective nouns*, eg crowd
>   *abstract nouns*, eg indignation, hysterics

Copy and complete the table to show which type of noun each word is.

Noun	Common	Proper	Collective	Abstract
family				
wainscoting				
candle				
vengeance				
Lord Canterville				
chains				
application				
Sir William Gull				
library				

Write a sentence using each of the nouns in the table above.

Adjectives

> *Adjectives* are words that describe or tell us more about a noun.
> Adjectives often describe a characteristic of the noun by its colour,
> smell, taste, feeling, sound or some other quality.

Using each of the adjectives below, write sentences of your own to illustrate
their meaning.

curious	feverish	ghastly	oblong	undisturbed	kaleidoscopic
matted	celebrated	antique	efficacious	motionless	uninterrupted

TEXT LEVEL WORK

Writing

Descriptive language

> The point of *descriptive language* in *The Canterville Ghost* is to describe
> the characters in such vivid detail that the reader can easily form an
> accurate and detailed impression of what is being written about.

Language features

Descriptive writing

You can do this by using:

- fresh and varied vocabulary
- descriptions of smell, sound, sight, touch and taste
- words that describe the quality of something, eg awful.

Detail

Specific detail is what makes writing more vivid and interesting.
You need to appeal directly to the reader's senses of:

- sight
- sound
- touch
- taste.
- smell

Precise choice of words

Use precise words to create a detailed understanding of the mood of the character, eg frightened, unconcerned, miserable etc. Adjectives, adverbs and verbs carry more emotion than nouns.

Below is a list of the words used to describe the ghost in the passage.
Copy and complete the table. For each word, tick the columns that indicate which senses are associated with the adjective. If the adjective does not appeal to the senses but to a quality, then explain what the quality is in the final column.

Adjective	Smell	Sound	Sight	Touch	Taste	Other comment
red						
burning						
long						
grey						
matted						
antique						
soiled						
ragged						
heavy						
rusty						
terrible						

With the help of a dictionary and thesaurus, find at least 10 new words associated with ghosts and haunting. Use these words in the writing assignment below.

Writing assignment

In the passage, the ghost remembers playing a number of different characters over the centuries. These include:

- the face at the window
- the skeleton
- the Green Hand
- Red Reuben
- the Strangled Babe
- Gaunt Gibeon, the Blood-sucker of Bexley Moor.

Choose one or more of these characters and write a description of them, using fresh and varied vocabulary which appeals to all five senses.

I heard a heavy step

Jonathan Harker is a young, newly qualified lawyer. His employers have sent him to Carpathia, in Transylvania, to be a legal adviser to Count Dracula, an eccentric nobleman. After a long, difficult and, at times, disturbing journey, Jonathan arrives at Dracula's castle.

I heard a heavy step approaching behind the great door, and saw through the chinks the gleam of a coming light. Then there was the sound of rattling chains and the clanking of massive bolts drawn back. A key was turned with the loud grating noise of long disuse, and the great door swung back.

Within, stood a tall old man, clean-shaven save for a long white moustache, and clad in black from head to foot, without a single speck of colour about him anywhere. He held in his hand an antique silver lamp, in which the flame burned without chimney or globe of any kind, throwing long, quivering shadows as it flickered in the draught of the open door. The old man motioned me in with his right hand with a courtly gesture, saying in excellent English, but with a strange intonation, 'Welcome to my house! Enter freely and of your own free will!' He made no motion of stepping to meet me, but stood like a statue, as though his gesture of welcome had fixed him into stone. The instant, however, that I had stepped over the threshold, he moved impulsively forward, and holding out his hand grasped mine with a strength which made me wince, an effect which was not lessened by the fact that it seemed cold as ice – more like the hand of a dead than a living man.

Again he said, 'Welcome to my house! Come freely. Go safely. And leave something of the happiness you bring!'

The strength of the handshake was so much akin to that which I had noticed in the driver, whose face I had not seen, that for a moment I doubted if it were not the same person to whom I was speaking; so to make sure, I said interrogatively, 'Count Dracula?'

He bowed in a courtly way as he replied, 'I am Dracula, and I bid you welcome, Mr. Harker, to my house. Come in; the night air is chill, and you must need to eat and rest.' As he was speaking, he put the lamp on a bracket on the wall, and stepping out, took my luggage; he had carried it in before I could forestall him. I protested, but he insisted, 'Nay, sir, you are my guest. It is late, and my people are not available. Let me see to your comfort myself.' He insisted on carrying my traps along the passage, and then up a great winding stair, and along another great passage, on whose stone floor our steps rang heavily. At the end of this he threw open a heavy door, and I rejoiced to see within a well-lit room in which a table was spread for supper, and on whose mighty hearth a great fire of logs flamed and flared.

The Count halted, putting down my bags, closed the door, and crossing the room, opened another door, which led into a small octagonal room lit by a single lamp, and seemingly without a window of any sort. Passing through this, he opened another door, and motioned me to enter. It was a welcome sight; for here was a great bedroom well lighted and warmed with another log fire, which sent a hollow roar up the wide chimney. The Count himself left my luggage inside and withdrew, saying, before he closed the door, 'You will need, after your journey, to refresh yourself by making your toilet. I trust you will find all you wish. When you are ready, come into the other room, where you will find your supper prepared.'

The light and warmth and the Count's courteous welcome seemed to have dissipated all my doubts and fears. Having then reached my normal state, I discovered that I was half-famished with hunger; so making a hasty toilet, I went into the other room.

I found supper already laid out. My host, who stood on one side of the great fireplace, leaning against the stone-work, made a graceful wave of his hand to the table, and said, 'I pray you, be seated and sup how you please. You will, I trust, excuse me that I do not join you; but I have dined already, and I do not sup.'

I handed to him the sealed letter which Mr. Hawkins had entrusted to me. He opened it and read it gravely; then, with a charming smile, he handed it to me to read. One passage of it, at least, gave me a thrill of pleasure:—

'I must regret that an attack of gout, from which malady I am a constant sufferer, forbids absolutely any travelling on my part for some time to come; but I am happy to say I can send a sufficient substitute, one in whom I have every possible confidence. He is a young man, full of energy and talent in his own way, and of a very faithful disposition. He is discreet and silent, and has grown into manhood in my service. He shall be ready to attend on you when you will during his stay, and shall take your instructions in all matters.'

The Count himself came forward and took off the cover of a dish, and I fell to at once on an excellent roast chicken. This, with some cheese and a salad and a bottle of old Tokay, of which I had two glasses, was my supper. During the time I was eating it the Count asked me many questions as to my journey, and I told him by degrees all I had experienced.

By this time I had finished my supper, and by my host's desire had drawn up a chair by the fire and begun to smoke a cigar which he offered me, at the same time excusing himself that he did not smoke. I had now an opportunity of observing him, and found him of a very marked physiognomy.

His face was a strong – a very strong – aquiline, with high bridge of the thin nose and peculiarly arched nostrils; with lofty domed forehead, and hair growing scantily round the temples, but profusely elsewhere. His eyebrows were very massive, almost meeting over the nose, and with bushy hair that seemed to curl in its own profusion. The mouth, so far as I could see it under the heavy moustache, was fixed and rather cruel-looking, with peculiarly sharp white teeth; these protruded over the lips, whose remarkable ruddiness showed astonishing vitality in a man of his years. For the rest, his ears were pale, and at the tops extremely pointed; the chin was broad and strong, and the cheeks firm though thin. The general effect was one of extraordinary pallor.

Hitherto I had noticed the backs of his hands as they lay on his knees in the firelight, and they had seemed rather white and fine; but seeing them now close to me, I could not but notice that they were rather coarse – broad, with squat fingers. Strange to say, there were hairs in the centre of the palm. The nails were long and fine, and cut to a sharp point. As the Count leaned over me and his hands touched me, I could not repress a shudder. It may have been that his breath was rank, but a horrible feeling of nausea came over me, which, do what I would, I could not conceal. The Count, evidently noticing it, drew back; and with a grim sort of smile, which showed more than he had yet done his protuberant teeth, sat himself down again on his own side of the fireplace. We were both silent for a while; and as I looked towards the window I saw the first dim streak of the coming dawn. There seemed a strange stillness over everything; but as I listened I heard, as if from down below in the valley, the howling of many wolves. The Count's eyes gleamed, and he said, 'Listen to them, the children of the night. What music they make!' Seeing, I suppose, some expression in my face strange to him, he added, 'Ah, sir, you dwellers in the city cannot enter into the feelings of the hunter.'

Bram Stoker

TEXT LEVEL WORK

Comprehension

A 1 Find three details from the passage which suggest that Count Dracula's home is large and imposing.

   2 What colour hair do you think Dracula has?

   3 Which details in the text suggest that the story is set in the past?

   4 What ailment prevented Mr Harker's employer from travelling to Carpathia himself?

   5 What is the name of Jonathan Harker's employer?

B 1 Which details in the text give the impression that Count Dracula is no ordinary man?

   2 What does Dracula mean when he says, '*It is late, and my people are not available*'?

   3 What does Jonathan Harker mean when he refers to his '*traps*'?

   4 What do you think is meant by the phrase '*old Tokay*'?

5 What detail reveals that Mr Harker must have reached the castle in the middle of the night?

C 1 Why do you think that Jonathan Harker felt uneasy with the Count?

2 What does Count Dracula mean when he refers to the 'children of the night' and their 'music' ?

3 Which details of Dracula's appearance make him seem strange to Jonathan Harker?

WORD LEVEL WORK

Vocabulary

Dictionary work
Use a dictionary and the context of the passage to explain the meanings of these words.

1 wince
2 interrogatively
3 replenished
4 dissipated
5 malady
6 physiognomy
7 courteous
8 pallor
9 discreet
10 aquiline
11 profusion
12 protuberant

HINT

HINT 1. Long words usually have a dominant syllable, one that has a natural high or low, or is more pronounced or stressed than the others, eg pro – <u>tub</u> – er – ant.

HINT 2. The number of vowel sounds tells you the number of syllables in a word. Even though there are two vowels in 'head', there is only one vowel sound.

HINT 3. When two consonants separate two vowel sounds, the first syllable usually ends after the first consonant, eg wel – come.

Spelling

Vowels and consonants

We can *spell* long words by blending sounds into syllables and then the syllables into words.
For example, in 'malady', the word is made up of three syllables:

mal – a – dy.

A *syllable* is a word or part of a word (a little chunk of a bigger word), containing one vowel sound.

Copy and complete the following table of words from the passage.
The first one has been done for you.

	Hint 1	Hint 2	Hint 3
protuberant	stress on <u>tub</u>	4 vowel sounds	pro/tub/er/ant
moustache			
massive			
gleam			
chimney			
intonation			
bracket			
gout			
famished			
draught			
threshold			

SENTENCE LEVEL WORK

Grammar and punctuation

Prepositions

> The word *preposition* is made up of two parts, 'pre' and 'position'.
> This gives the clue that prepositions are about the position of something
> (a noun). The most common prepositions of place and movement are:
>
> > *in*   *at*   *on*   and   *to*.
>
> Prepositions can also be about time:
>
> > *at*   *on*   and   *in*.
>
> You use *in / into*:
>
> - with spaces, eg in a castle, in a bedroom, in a forest, in a park
> - with bodies of water, eg in the water, in the river, in the sea
> - with lines, eg in a row, in a line, in a queue
>
> You use *at*:
>
> - with places, eg at the door, at the theatre, at the school
> - with places on a page, eg at the top of the page
> - in groups of people, eg at the back of the class
>
> You use *on*:
>
> - with surfaces, eg on the wall, on the table
> - with small islands, eg on the Isle of Man
> - with directions, eg on the left, on the right
>
> You use *to* with verbs of movement such as go, come, drive: eg
> > go to work

A Copy these sentences and fill in the appropriate prepositions of place and movement.

1 He held ⌣ his hand an antique silver lamp.

2 He put the lamp ⌣ a bracket on the wall.

3 My host, who stood ⌣ one side of the great fireplace, leaning against the stonework, made a graceful wave of his hand ⌣ the table.

4 He handed it ⌣ me to read.

5 When you are ready, come ⌣ the other room.

B Copy the sentences and fill in the appropriate prepositions of time.

1 The carriage was due ⌣ midnight.

2 Jonathan Harker was arriving at the castle ⌣ Monday. Count Dracula was travelling to London ⌣ October.

3 Dracula slept in his coffin ⌣ the daytime.

4 ⌣ winter the wolves are more active.

5 Jonathan's predecessor had been committed to an asylum ⌣ August.

TEXT LEVEL WORK

Writing

Descriptive writing

> As a writer, you want your audience to hang on to your every word and to experience the scene exactly as you did. A really good *description* helps the reader or listener to feel the scene as well as to picture it. However, you need to create a full impression of a person, place or thing by using key elements of description in your writing to make it come alive.

Language features

Figurative language

Imagery (creating word pictures) is crucial in good descriptive writing. Figurative language includes the following:

- simile – a comparison using 'like' or 'as', eg he stood like a statue
- metaphor – a metaphor is like a simile but instead of saying one thing is like or as another it says one thing is or was another. In other words it makes a direct comparison, eg

  children of the night
- personification – giving inanimate objects or ideas human qualities, eg

  nausea came over me
- hyperbole – exaggeration. This is very effective for emphasis, eg

  without a single speck of colour about him.

Copy and complete the table by identifying the figures of speech with letters:

- S for simile
- M for metaphor
- P for personification
- H for hyperbole

Text	Figure of speech
1 a heavy step approaching	
2 throwing long quivering shadows	
3 cold as ice	
4 a table was spread	
5 music they make	
6 drawn up a chair	
7 dwellers in the city cannot enter into the feelings	

Writing assignment

Imagine you are Count Dracula. Write a description of Jonathan Harker after he has been with you some time, using some of the following details from the whole story in your description.

anxious to be punctual

speaks a little German

interested in superstitions

curious about mysteries

keen to please, sympathetic

engaged to Mina Hawkins

likes reading

likes good food and drink

did research on Transylvania

very observant

imaginative and impressionable

worked in Exeter and London

educated and intelligent

young, active and fit

Regeane went forward

The story takes place in ancient Rome, the city whose founders, Romulus and Remus, were raised by a she-wolf. A young girl, Regeane, is being kept imprisoned by her step-father (Gundabald) and step-brother (Hugo), following the death of her mother, Gisela. Regeane is imprisoned because she has a secret and that secret frightens those around her. Regeane herself does not fully understand what happens to her at the full moon.

Regeane went forward boldly, knowing that in a moment she would be warm. Naked, she stepped into the silver haze. The wolf stood there.

Regeane was, as wolves go, a large wolf. She had the same weight as the girl, over a hundred pounds. She was much stronger than in her human state – lean, quick, and powerful. Her coat was smooth and thick. The pelt glowed silver as it caught the moonlight on its long guard hairs.

The wolf's heart overflowed with joy and gratitude. Regeane would never have admitted it in her human state, but she loved the wolf and, papal blessing or not, she would never let the wolf go.

From the bottom of her heart, she revelled in the change. Sometimes, while in her human state, she wondered who was wiser, she or the wolf. The wolf knew. Growing more beautiful and stronger year after year, the wolf waited for Regeane to be ready to receive her teaching and understand it.

The silver wolf lifted herself on her hind legs and, placing her forepaws on the window sill, peered out. She saw not just with eyes as these maimed humans did, but with sensitive ears and nose.

The world humans saw was like a fresco – dimensionless as a picture painted on a wall. To be believed in by the wolf, a thing had to have not only image, but smell, texture, and taste.

Ah God ... how beautiful. The world was filled with wonder.

The rain must have come in the evening. The wolf could smell the damp, black earth under the green verdure as well as mud churned up by horses' hooves in a nearby lane.

The woman hadn't noticed it. She'd spent the day in grief-stricken reverie. For this she earned a brief flash of contempt from the wolf. But the wolf was too much a creature of the present to dwell on what was past. She was grateful for each moment. And this was a fine one.

Usually, in Rome, the scent of man overpowered everything else. That effluvia of stale perspiration, raw sewage floating in the Tiber, the stench of human excrement which, even by comparison to that of other animals, is utterly vile. All these filled the air and pressed in around her. Overlaying them were the musty omnipresent evidence of human dwellings: stale woodsmoke, damp timber, and stone.

But not tonight. The sharp wind blew from the open fields beyond the city, redolent of dry grass and the sweetness of wild herbs growing on the hillsides near the sea.

Sometimes the fragrant breath from the Campagna carried the clean barnyard smells of pig and cattle, and faintly, the enticing musk of deer.

The night below was alive with movement. The cats that made their homes among the ruins sang their ancient songs of anger and passion among forgotten monuments. Here and there the slinking shape of a stray dog met her eye; occasionally, even furtive human movement. Thieves and footpads haunted the district, ready to prey on the unwary.

Her ears pricked forward and netted what her eyes could not see – the suade thump of a barn owl's wings in flight, the high, thin cries of bats swooping, darting, foraging for insects in the chill night air.

The rush and whisper of the hunters and the hunted, silent until the end. The agonised death cry of a bird, taken in sleep on the nest by a marauding cat, rent the air. The chopped-off shriek of a rabbit dying in the talons of an owl followed.

Those and many others were woven together by her wolf senses into a rich fabric that was unending variety and everlasting delight.

The silver wolf dropped her forepaws to the floor with a soft, nearly inaudible cry of longing. Then her lips drew back from her teeth in a snarl at the sound of voices in the other room.

Hugo and Gundabald were eating. The wolf's belly rumbled with hunger at the smell of roast meat. She was hungry and thirsty, longing for clean water and food.

The woman warned her night side to rein in her desires. She would get nothing.

The wolf replied. They were both gone, the woman from her prison, the wolf from her cage. The wolf stood beside a clear mountain lake. The full moon glowed silver in the water. All around the lake, black trees were silhouetted against mountains glittering white with unending snow.

The memory faded. The wolf and the woman found themselves staring at the locked door.

The wolf and the woman both understood imprisonment. Regeane had spent most of her life behind locked doors. She'd long ago learned the punishing futility of assaults on oak and iron. She ignored what she couldn't change and bided her time.

They were speaking of her.

'Did you hear that?' Hugo asked fearfully. Hugo's ears were better than Gundbald's. He must have heard her soft cry of protest.

'No,' Gundbald mumbled through a mouthful of food. 'I didn't and you didn't either. You only imagined you did. She seldom makes any noise. That's one thing we can be grateful for. At least she doesn't spend her nights howling as a real wolf would.'

'We shouldn't have brought her here,' Hugo moaned.

'Must you start that again?' Gundabald sighed wearily.

'It's true,' Hugo replied with drunken insistence. 'The founders of this city were suckled at the tits of a mother wolf. Once they called themselves sons of the wolf. Ever since I found out about her I've often thought of that story. A real wolf couldn't raise human children, but a creature like her ...'.   *Alice Borchadt*

TEXT LEVEL WORK

Comprehension

A 1 What is meant by the '*silver haze*' in the opening paragraph?

  2 What is meant by the word '*fresco*'?

  3 Why is Regeane described as having spent the day grief-stricken?

  4 Why has Regeane been imprisoned by Gundabald?

B 1 What do we learn about the city of Rome, from the wolf's senses?

  2 What memory does the wolf have of her time in the mountains?

  3 Why does Hugo associate Regeane with the founders of the city of Rome?

  4 What impression does the writer create of the wolf's senses?

C 1 Why does the writer state that, '*The wolf and the woman both understood imprisonment*'?

  2 In what ways is the passage a successful description of a woman changing into a werewolf, and in what ways is it less successful?

WORD LEVEL WORK

Vocabulary

Dictionary work

Use a dictionary and the context of the passage to explain the meaning of the following words.

1 lean	4 verdure	7 effluvia	10 slinking
2 pelt	5 reverie	8 omnipresent	11 furtive
3 maimed	6 contempt	9 redolent	12 footpads

Spelling

Vowel sounds

> The vowel combinations *ie* and *ei* can be confusing. Here are the rules:
> *i* comes before *e* when the sound is *ee* , eg
>
>   gr<u>ie</u>f   bel<u>ie</u>ve
>
> But *i* does not come before *e* when it follows a *c* , eg
>
>   rec<u>ei</u>ve   c<u>ei</u>ling
>
> And *i* does not come before *e* when the sound is not *ee* , eg
>
>   w<u>ei</u>ght   v<u>ei</u>l

A Copy these headings and put the words below in the correct column.

ie = ee sound	ei = follows a c	ei = sound not ee

thieves	shriek	rein	chief	their
leisure	deceive	receipt	eight	deceit
retrieve	brief	wield	priest	field
shield	heir	sovereign	foreign	conceit

HINT
Use a dictionary to find the meaning of any words you do not know.

B There are always exceptions to spelling rules. Learn these!

protein	weird	seize
plebeian	weir	species

SENTENCE LEVEL WORK

Grammar and punctuation

Conjunctions

Conjunctions are words that are used to join two sentences.
The two conjunctions we use most often are *and* and *but*.

'She ignored what she couldn't change.' 'She bided her time.'

'She ignored what she couldn't change **and** bided her time.'

'She was hungry and thirsty. She knew she would get nothing.'

'She was hungry and thirsty **but** she knew she would get nothing.'

Conjunctions which are placed between the sentences that they join
are called *coordinating conjunctions*.

You can remember these simple conjunctions by using
the word FANBOYS.

F	A	N	B	O	Y	S
for	and	nor	but	or	yet	so

A Copy these sentences and fill in the missing conjunctions, using five of the seven words above.

1 Gundabald had tickets for the amphitheatre *for* the races.

2 The gladiators rehearse on Tuesday *and* the chariots practise on Wednesday.

3 Have you seen *and* heard the play by Seneca?

4 Hugo wanted to sit near the emperor's balcony __ he ordered his tickets early.

5 Regeane walked into the moonlight as a woman *so* she emerged as a wolf.

TEXT LEVEL WORK

Writing

Descriptive writing

Remember! *Descriptive writing* needs:

- fresh and varied vocabulary
- interesting comparisons – simile, metaphors
- descriptions of smell, sound, sight, touch and taste – hyperbole, onomatopoeia
- words that describe the quality of something, eg awful

Language features

Dominant impression

Think of how you want your reader to feel by your description, eg frightened, happy, sad etc. This is the *dominant impression* you need to create.

Sound devices

These help to develop descriptions, using the sense of sound. They create atmosphere and give writing a feeling of rhythm.

- alliteration – the repetition of consonant sounds, such as 'the wolves howled weirdly'
- assonance – the repetition of vowel sounds, such as 'he climbed briskly into the interior'
- onomatopoeia – words that imitate sounds, such as 'plop', 'crunch', or 'buzz'.

For example:

'the slinking shape of a stray dog' – here the 's' sound is repeated, ie alliteration

'the wolf and the woman both understood imprisonment' – here the 'o' is repeated, ie assonance

'thump' – here the word sounds like the noise it describes, ie onomatopoeia.

Time

Take your reader through the description of your character in a chronological way. Compare 'before' and 'after' situations to show changes in physical appearance and character.

Writing assignment

Write a description of a person changing into a werewolf. The details below will give you some ideas to get you started but you may need a dictionary to help you.

Details for senses
Sight
face contorted in pain / subtly shaded silver pelt / delicate pink tongue ears twitching alertly / racked by spasms / lithe and powerful body / grotesque smoothly rippling muscles / penetrating amber eyes / painfully bright shaft of light
Smell
musky animal smell / rank-smelling breath / delicate odour of lilies
Hearing
bone-wrenching convulsions / sibilant whispering / muffled thump lips drawn back in a snarl / piercing shrieks
Taste
metallic taste of blood / cloying sweet taste of flesh
Touch
grating rasp of stone on skin / bruising blows on bone / skin-crawling shudders
Figurative language
this is madness / sodden with suffering / in blind panic / wolf prowled in her brain their eyes locked / ridged like broken stone / hatred and malice hovered blind, murderous rage

They murdered him

They murdered him.

As he turned to take the ball, a dam burst against the side of his head and a hand grenade shattered his stomach. Engulfed by nausea, he pitched towards the grass. His mouth encountered gravel, and he spat frantically, afraid that some of his teeth had been knocked out. Rising to his feet, he saw the field through drifting gauze but held on until everything settled into place, like a lens focusing, making the world sharp again, with edges.

The second play called for a pass. Fading back, he picked up a decent block and cocked his arm, searching for a receiver – maybe the tall kid they called The Goober. Suddenly, he was caught from behind and whirled violently, a toy boat caught in the whirlpool. Landing on his knees, hugging the ball, he urged himself to ignore the pain that gripped his groin, knowing that it was important to betray no sign of distress, remembering The Goober's advice, 'Coach is testing you, testing, and he's looking for guts.'

I've got guts, Jerry murmured, getting up by degrees, careful not to displace any of his bones or sinews. A telephone rang in his ears. Hallo, hallo, I'm still here. When he moved his lips, he tasted the acid of dirt and grass and gravel. He was aware of the other players around him, helmeted and grotesque, creatures from an unknown world. He had never felt so lonely in his life, abandoned, defenceless.

On the third play, he was hit simultaneously by three of them: one, his knees; another his stomach; a third, his head – his helmet no protection at all. His body seemed to telescope into itself but all the parts didn't fit, and he was stunned by the knowledge that pain isn't just one thing – it is cunning and various, sharp here and sickening there, burning here and clawing there. He clutched himself as he hit the ground. The ball squirted away. His breath went away, like the ball – a terrible stillness pervaded him – and then, at the onset of panic, his breath came back again. His lips sprayed wetness and he was grateful for the sweet cool air that filled his lungs. But when he tried to get up, his body mutinied against movement. He decided the hell with it. He'd go to sleep right here, right out on the fifty-yard line, the hell with trying out for the team, screw everything, he was going to sleep, he didn't care any more.

'Renault!'

Ridiculous, someone calling his name.

'Renault!'

The coach's voice scraped like sandpaper against his ears. He opened his eyes flutteringly. 'I'm all right,' he said to nobody in particular, or to his father maybe. Or the coach. He was unwilling to abandon this lovely lassitude but he had to, of course. He was sorry to leave the earth, and he was vaguely curious about how he was going to get up, with both legs smashed and his skull battered in. He was astonished to find himself on his feet, intact, bobbing like one of those toy novelties dangling from car windows, but erect.

'For Christ's sake,' the coach bellowed, his voice juicy with contempt. A spurt of saliva hit Jerry's cheek.

Hey coach, you spit on me, Jerry protested. Stop the spitting, coach. What he said aloud was, 'I'm all right, coach,' because he was a coward about stuff like that, thinking one thing and saying another, planning one thing and doing another – he had been Peter a thousand times and a thousand cocks had crowed in his lifetime.

'How tall are you, Renault?'

'Five nine,' he gasped, still fighting for breath.

'Weight?'

'One forty-five,' he said, looking the coach straight in the eye.

'Soaking wet, I'll bet,' the coach said sourly. 'What the hell you want to play football for? You need more meat on those bones. What the hell you trying to play quarterback for? You'd make a better end. Maybe.'

The coach looked like an old gangster: broken nose, a scar on his cheek like a stitched shoestring. He needed a shave, his stubble like slivers of ice. He growled and swore and was merciless. But a helluva coach, they said. The coach stared at him now, the dark eyes probing, pondering. Jerry hung in there, trying not to sway, trying not to faint.

'All right,' the coach said in disgust. 'Show up tomorrow. Three o'clock sharp or you're through before you start.'

Inhaling the sweet sharp apple air through his nostrils he was afraid to open his mouth wide, wary of any movement that was not absolutely essential – he walked tentatively towards the sidelines, listening to the coach barking at the other guys. Suddenly, he loved that voice. 'Show up tomorrow.'

He trudged away from the field, blinking against the afternoon sun, towards the locker room at the gym. His knees were liquid and his body light as air, suddenly.

Know what? He asked himself, a game he played sometimes.

What?

I'm going to make the team.

Dreamer, dreamer.

Not a dream: it's the truth.

Robert Cormier

TEXT LEVEL WORK

Comprehension

A 1 What sport is Jerry taking part in?

2 When Jerry Renault hit the gravel, what was he afraid had happened?

3 When the coach spoke to Jerry, what did he want to know?

4 What time does Jerry have to show up tomorrow?

5 What is Jerry's '*dream*'?

B 1 In which country do you think the story is set?

2 Why does Jerry know that '*It was important to show no signs of distress*'?

3 What is really happening when we are told that 'A telephone rang in his ears'?

4 Why do you think the other players appear to Jerry as 'creatures from an unknown world'?

5 What do you think the author means when he writes 'He had been Peter a thousand times and a thousand cocks had crowed in his lifetime'?

C 1 After reading the first paragraph of the passage what did you think the story was going to be about?

2 Write down some words and phrases from the first paragraph which gave you this impression.

3 Why do you think the writer begins the story in this way?

WORD LEVEL WORK

Vocabulary

Dictionary work

Use a dictionary and the context of the extract to explain the meaning of the following words.

1 engulfed	5 simultaneously	9 intact
2 distress	6 pervaded	10 merciless
3 grotesque	7 mutinied	11 pondering
4 abandoned	8 lassitude	12 tentatively

Spelling

Prefixes

A *prefix* is a group of letters put at the beginning of a word to change its meaning, eg

un + known = unknown

pre + view = preview

The spelling rule is simple. Just add the prefix!

A Copy these words and underline the prefixes.

1 immigrant	4 return	7 nonsense
2 disassemble	5 unwise	8 mistake
3 misbehave	6 interactive	9 anticlockwise

B Use a dictionary to help you write three words with each of these prefixes.

1 un

2 in

3 mis

SENTENCE LEVEL WORK

Grammar and punctuation

Sentence types

> A *sentence* is a group of words which makes sense, eg
>
> 'The second player called for a pass.'
>
> 'A telephone rang in his ears.'
>
> There are three main types of sentences:
>
> statements 'I'm going to make the team.'
> questions 'How tall are you, Renault?'
> exclamations 'Renault!'
>
> For each type of sentence you must begin with a capital letter.
> Statements end with a *full stop*.
> Questions end with *question marks*.
> Exclamations end with *exclamation marks*.

HINT

Notice that both the question mark and the exclamation mark have a built-in full stop.

A Copy and punctuate these sentences correctly.

1 jerry was trying out for the football team

2 he opened his eyes flutteringly

3 stop that spitting

4 how much do you weigh

5 i'm going to get really hurt

6 what time did Jerry have to return the next day

HINT

Remember the capital letters.

B Write three questions you might want to ask Jerry after he has made the team.

TEXT LEVEL WORK

Writing

Story openings

> Robert Cormier begins his story *The Chocolate War* by giving the reader the impression that Jerry Renault is involved in some sort of war situation.
>
> There are a few clues, such as the words 'ball' and 'field', but the reader almost doesn't notice them in the impression of a battleground that is created.
>
> It appears that the *story opening* is giving the reader the wrong impression but, as we read on, we see that the violence on the football field fits in with the impression of war that has been created.

Language features

Opening sentence

The very short opening sentence, '*They murdered him*', is designed to interest the reader and keep us guessing:

Who are 'they'?

Who has been 'murdered'?

Just what is going on?

Creating an impression

The writer deliberately leads the reader into thinking one thing when, in actual fact, something totally different is going on. We read on and are surprised.

The writer's intention is to draw a comparison between one activity (war) and another activity (football) so, as we read, we can appreciate just how violent the game is.

Writing in the third person

Many stories are told by a 'narrator'. The narrator is not a character in the story. He/she is the storyteller and

- relates what is happening in the story   ie the plot
- helps the reader to get to know the people in the story   ie the characters
- describes where the story takes place   ie the setting.

Writing assignment

Write the first two paragraphs of a story where:

- the first paragraph leads the reader into thinking that something is happening
- the second paragraph shows the reader that, in actual fact, something that they would never have guessed is actually happening.

Remember:

- a short opening sentence is needed to 'grab' the reader's interest
- the two 'activities' must have something in common. In *The Chocolate War*, the common theme is violence.
- to write in the third person so you, as the narrator, can create the 'wrong' impression for the reader and then explain what is really going on.

Personal choice

Choose one of the following assignments.

1 Write a character description of Jerry. You will have to imagine what he looks like but there are clues in the story opening to help you understand what sort of boy he is.

2 Write a paragraph to explain why you would, or would not, like to read the rest of this story.

Last night I dreamt

Last night I dreamt I went to Manderley again. It seemed to me I stood by the iron gate leading to the drive, and for a while I could not enter for the way was barred to me. There was a padlock and a chain upon the gate. I called in my dream to the lodge-keeper, and had no answer, and peering closer through the rusted spokes of the gate I saw that the lodge was uninhabited.

No smoke came from the chimney, and the little lattice windows gaped forlorn. Then, like all dreamers, I was possessed of a sudden with supernatural powers and passed like a spirit through the barrier before me. The drive wound away in front of me, twisting and turning as it had always done, but as I advanced I was aware that a change had come upon it; it was narrow and unkept, not the drive that we had known. At first I was puzzled and did not understand, and it was only when I bent my head to avoid the low swinging branch of a tree that I realised what had happened. Nature had come into her own again and, little by little, in her stealthy, insidious way had encroached upon the drive with long, tenacious fingers. The woods, always a menace even in the past, had triumphed

in the end. They crowded, dark and uncontrolled, to the borders of the drive. The beeches with white, naked limbs leant close to one another, their branches intermingled in a strange embrace, making a vault above my head like the archway of a church. And there were other trees as well, trees that I did not recognise, squat oaks and tortured elms that straggled cheek by jowl with the beeches, and had thrust themselves out of the quiet earth, along with monster shrubs and plants, none of which I remembered.

The drive was a ribbon now, a thread of its former self, with gravel surface gone, and choked with grass and moss. The trees had thrown out low branches, making an impediment to progress; the gnarled roots looked like skeleton claws. Scattered here and again amongst this jungle growth, I would recognise shrubs that had been land-marks in our time, things of culture and of grace, hydrangeas whose blue heads had been famous. No hand had checked their progress, and they had gone native now, rearing to monster height without a bloom, black and ugly as the nameless parasites that grew beside them.

On and on, now east now west, wound the poor thread that had once been our drive. Sometimes I thought it lost, but it appeared again, beneath a fallen tree perhaps, or struggling on the other side of a muddied ditch created by the winter rains. I had not thought the way so long. Surely the miles had multiplied, even as the trees had done, and the path led but to a labyrinth, some choked wilderness, and not to the house at all. I came upon it suddenly; the approach masked by the unnatural growth of a vast shrub that spread in all directions, and I stood, my heart thumping in my breast, the strange prick of tears behind my eyes.

There was Manderley, our Manderley, secretive and silent as it had always been, the grey stone shining in the moonlight of my dream, the mullioned windows reflecting the green lawns and the terrace. Time could not wreck the perfect symmetry of those walls, nor the site itself, a jewel in the hollow of a hand.

The terrace sloped to the lawns, and the lawns stretched to the sea, and turning I could see the sheet of silver, placid under the moon, like a lake undisturbed by wind or storm. No waves would come to ruffle this dream water, and no bulk of cloud, wind-driven from the west, obscure the clarity of this pale sky. I turned again to the house, and though it stood inviolate, untouched, as though we ourselves had left but yesterday, I saw that the garden had obeyed the jungle law, even as the woods had done. The rhododendrons stood fifty feet high, twisted and entwined with bracken, and they had entered into an alien marriage with a host of nameless shrubs, poor, bastard things that clung to their roots as though conscious of their spurious origin. A lilac had mated with a copper beech, and to bind them yet more closely to one another, the malevolent ivy, always an enemy to grace, had thrown her tendrils about the pair and made them prisoners. Ivy held prior place in this lost garden, the long strands crept across the lawns, and soon would encroach upon the house itself. There was another plant too, some half-breed from the woods, whose seed had been scattered long ago beneath the trees and then forgotten, and now, marching in unison with the ivy, thrust its ugly form like a giant rhubarb towards the soft grass where the daffodils had blown.

Nettles were everywhere, the van-guard of the army. They choked the terrace, they sprawled about the paths, they leant, vulgar and lanky, against the very windows of the house. They made indifferent sentinels, for in many places their ranks had been broken by the rhubarb plant, and they lay with crumpled heads and listless stems, making a pathway for the rabbits. I left the drive and went on to the terrace, for the nettles were no barrier to me, a dreamer, I walked enchanted, and nothing held me back.

Moonlight can play odd tricks upon the fancy, even upon a dreamer's fancy. As I stood there, hushed and still, I could swear that the house was not an empty shell but lived and breathed as it had lived before.

Light came from the windows, the curtains blew softly in the night air, and there, in the library, the door would stand half open as we had left it, with my handkerchief on the table beside the bowl of autumn roses.

Daphne du Maurier

TEXT LEVEL WORK

Comprehension

A 1 Why couldn't the writer pass through the iron gate?

2 In your own words, explain what changes had come over the drive.

3 What simile describes how the branches of the beech trees had grown together?

4 What impression does the writer give of the state of the lawns?

5 What 'trick' does the moonlight play upon the writer?

> **HINT**
>
> A simile is a comparison, eg *as white as snow.*

B 1 Find and quote five examples of descriptive words and phrases which give the impression that Manderley has long been deserted.

2 Explain in your own words:

   a. '*like all dreamers I was possessed of a sudden with supernatural powers*'

   b. '*Nature had come into her own again.*'

3 What evidence is there in the text to suggest that the dreamer has been to Manderley before?

4 The writer describes her feelings as she comes upon the house:

   '*I stood, my heart thumping in my breast, the strange prick of tears behind my eyes.*'

   Why do you think she feels this way?

5 In what way do the final two paragraphs contrast with what has gone before?

C What are your thoughts about the opening of this story? Does it make you want to read the story or not? Give your opinion and explain your reasons.

WORD LEVEL WORK

Vocabulary

Dictionary work

Use a dictionary and the context in the story opening to explain the meaning of these words.

1 uninhabited
2 forlorn
3 insidious
4 encroached
5 tenacious
6 impediment

7 labyrinth
8 symmetry
9 placid
10 inviolate
11 van-guard
12 sentinels

Spelling

Prefixes

A *prefix* is a group of letters put at the beginning of a word to change its meaning. Many prefixes make the word into its opposite, eg

inhabited	un + inhabited
controlled	un + controlled
famous	in + famous

A Choose a prefix from the box to make each of the following words into its opposite.

> un   mis   dis   im

1 tidy
2 appear
3 possible

4 count
5 wrap
6 obey

7 lead
8 moral
9 true

B Use a dictionary to find three words beginning with the following prefixes:

anti
over

Write the word and its opposite. The first one has been done for you.

anti	over
1 anticlimax / climax	1
2	2
3	3

SENTENCE LEVEL WORK

Grammar and punctuation

Subject and verb

> Every sentence has a *subject* – the person, place or thing that the sentence is about.
>
> Every sentence has to have a *verb*.
> The subject of the sentence is the person or thing that is doing the action of the verb, eg
>
> 'The terrace sloped to the lawns.'
>   subject verb

A Copy and complete the table by writing in the subject and verb from each of the sentences 1 to 5 below. The first one has been done for you.

Sentence	Subject	Verb
1	I	had
2		

1 I had a wonderful dream.
2 The drive wound away in front of me.
3 The house was secretive and silent.
4 The rhododendrons stood fifty feet high.
5 The nettles choked the terrace.

TEXT LEVEL WORK

Writing

Story openings

> It is very important to have an interesting *story opening* so the reader will want to 'read on'. The opening of *Rebecca* is very mysterious and leaves many unanswered questions:
>
> Who is the dreamer? Why does she return to Manderley in her dream? Why is the house deserted?
>
> This story opening is very descriptive. It is written in the first person.

Language features

Writing in the first person

The writer of the story is recounting what happened:

'*I called in my dream to the lodge-keeper ...*'

and how she felt:

'*At first I was puzzled and did not understand ...*'

When you write in the first person you should avoid starting every sentence with 'I', which can become boring. You can change the order of the words, eg

'I dreamt last night I went to Manderley again.'

'**Last night** I dreamt I went to Manderley again.'

You can use conjunctions to join sentences, eg

'I was possessed of a sudden with supernatural powers.' 'I passed like a spirit through the barrier before me.'

'I was possessed of a sudden with supernatural powers **and** passed like a spirit through the barrier before me.'

Improve this piece of writing by changing the order of the words and using conjunctions.

> I had a dream last night. I was in a huge wood. I didn't recognise the place. I was sure I had never been there before. I didn't feel frightened. I was very cold. I walked through the wood. I came to an old house. I decided to go inside. I woke up.

Descriptive writing

It is important if you are writing a descriptive story opening that your reader can 'see' the place you are describing. Compare these two sentences:

'The house stood on the edge of the wood.'

'The house, ruined and deserted, stood on the edge of the dark, forbidding wood.'

The second sentence has used the adjectives 'dark', and 'forbidding' and an adjectival phrase, 'ruined and deserted', to help the reader imagine the scene.

Use adjectives and adjectival phrases to improve these sentences.

1 The drive led to the house.
2 The window was open.
3 The lawn sloped down to the sea.
4 There were rose bushes in the garden.
5 The gate was unlocked.

Writing assignment

Write a story opening which begins with a dream. Remember:

- write in the first person
- the dream can be real or imaginary
- the opening describes the scene where the rest of the story will take place
- in the dream you visit a place from your past
- this place can be eerie and frightening or warm and welcoming
- to use descriptive words and phrases so that your reader has a clear picture of the place you have visited in your dream
- avoid beginning every sentence with 'I'.

Personal choice

Choose one of the following assignments.

1 The person telling the story has come back to Manderley in her dream, many years after she has lived there. She describes how the garden is overgrown and neglected. Imagine that the inside of the house is the same as no one has looked after it for years. Write a description of one of the rooms in the house as she sees it in her dream.

2 Write a paragraph to say why you would, or would not like to read the rest of this story.

As Gregor Samsa awoke

As Gregor Samsa awoke one morning from uneasy dreams he found himself transformed in his bed into a gigantic insect. He was lying on his hard, as it were armour-plated, back and when he lifted his head a little he could see his dome-like brown belly divided into stiff arched segments on top of which the bed-quilt could hardly keep in position and was about to slide off completely. His numerous legs, which were pitifully thin compared to the rest of his bulk, waved helplessly before his eyes.

What has happened to me? he thought. It was no dream. His room, a regular human bedroom, only rather too small, lay quiet between the four familiar walls. Above the table on which a collection of cloth samples was unpacked and spread out – Samsa was a commercial traveller – hung the picture which he had recently cut out of an illustrated magazine and put into a pretty gilt frame. It showed a lady, with a fur cap on and a fur stole, sitting upright and holding out to the spectator a huge fur muff into which the whole of her forearm had vanished.

Gregor's eyes turned next to the window, and the overcast sky – one could hear raindrops beating on the window gutter – made him quite melancholy. What about sleeping a little longer and forgetting all this nonsense, he thought, but it could not be done, for he was accustomed to sleep on his right side and in his present condition he could not turn himself over. However violently he forced himself towards his right side he always rolled on to his back again. He tried it at least a hundred times, shutting his eyes to keep from seeing his struggling legs, and only desisted when he began to feel in his side a faint dull ache he had never experienced before.

O God, he thought, what an exhausting job I've picked on! Travelling about day in, day out. It's much more irritating work than doing the actual business in the warehouse, and on top of that there's the trouble of constant travelling, of worrying about train connections, the bed and irregular meals, casual acquaintances that are always new and never become intimate friends. The devil take it all! He felt a slight itching up on his belly; slowly pushed himself on his back nearer to the top of the bed so that he could lift his head more easily, identified the itching place which was surrounded by many small white spots the nature of which he could not understand, and made to touch it with a leg, but drew the leg back immediately, for the contact made a cold shiver go through him...

He looked at the alarm-clock ticking on the chest. Heavenly Father! he thought. It was half past six o'clock and the hands were quietly moving on, it was even past the half hour, it was getting on for a quarter to seven. Had the alarm-clock not gone off? From the bed one could see that it had been properly set for four o'clock; of course it must have gone off. Yes, but was it possible to sleep quietly through that ear-splitting noise? Well, he had not slept quietly, yet apparently all the more soundly for that. But what was he to do now? The next train went at seven o'clock; to catch that he would need to hurry like mad and his samples weren't even packed up, and he himself wasn't feeling particularly fresh and active. And even if he did catch the train he wouldn't avoid a row with the chief, since the warehouse porter would have been waiting for the five o'clock train and would have long since reported his failure to turn up. The porter was a creature of the chief's, spineless and stupid. Well, supposing he were to say he was sick? But that would be most unpleasant and would look suspicious, since during his five years' employment he had not been ill once. The chief himself would be sure to come with the sick-insurance doctor, would reproach his parents with their son's laziness, and would cut all excuses short by referring to the insurance doctor, who of course regarded all mankind as perfectly healthy malingerers. And would he be so far wrong on this occasion? Gregor really felt quite well, apart from a drowsiness that was utterly superfluous after such a long sleep, and he was even unusually hungry.

As all this was running through his mind at top speed without his being able to decide to leave his bed – the alarm-clock had just struck a quarter to seven – there came a cautious tap at the door behind the head of the bed. 'Gregor,' said a voice – it was his mother's – 'it's a quarter to seven. Hadn't you a train to catch?' That gentle voice! Gregor had a shock as he heard his own voice answering hers, unmistakably his own voice, it was true, but with a persistent horrible twittering squeak behind it like an undertone, that left the words in their clear shape only for the first moment and then rose up reverberating round them to destroy their sense, so that one could not be sure one had heard them rightly. Gregor wanted to answer at length and explain everything, but in the circumstances he confined himself to saying: 'Yes, yes, thank you, mother, I'm getting up now.' The wooden door between them must have kept the change in his voice from being noticeable outside, for his mother contented herself with this statement and shuffled away.

Franz Kafka

TEXT LEVEL WORK

Comprehension

A 1 When Gregor woke up, what unusual thing had happened?

2 What does Gregor do for a living?

3 Why couldn't he go back to sleep and *'forget all this nonsense'*?

4 What does Gregor think about as he is lying on his back, unable to move?

5 Who comes to find out why Gregor has not yet got up?

B 1 What do you think Gregor's *'uneasy dreams'* were about?

2 Why is Gregor sure that what is happening is *'no dream'*?

3 What do you think the writer means when he says *'the porter was a creature of the chief's'*?

4 What sort of relationship to you think Gregor has with:
   - the porter?
   - the chief?

5 What *'shock'* does Gregor get in the final paragraph of the extract?

C 1 What do you think of the opening sentence? How did it make you feel?

2 Gregor wakes up to discover he is an insect. He then goes on to think about everyday things.

Would you expect someone who has woken up as an insect to behave like this?

How might you have expected him to behave?

WORD LEVEL WORK

Vocabulary

Dictionary work

Use a dictionary and the context of the extract to explain the meaning of these words.

1 uneasy	5 desisted	9 malingerers
2 transformed	6 intimate	10 superfluous
3 segments	7 spineless	11 cautious
4 melancholy	8 suspicious	12 persistent

Spelling

Prefixes

A *prefix* is a group of letters put at the beginning of a word to change its meaning. Many prefixes make the word into its opposite.

The spelling rule for prefixes is simple. Just add it!
Sometimes the last letter of the prefix is the same as the first letter of the word you are adding it to, eg

di**s** + satisfied = di**ss**atisfied
i**r** + regular = i**rr**egular

This creates a double letter. Don't leave one of them out!

An unusual prefix is **al**. It comes from the word 'all' meaning total, or whole amount, but be careful! When you add it to the front of a word it only has one 'l', eg

all + most = **al**most
all + ways = **al**ways.

Copy each of these words and add the prefix. Watch your spelling!

dis +	appear	service	similar
	honest	soluble	satisfy
un +	natural	packed	needed
	necessary	pleasant	numbered
over +	age	run	cast
	rule	ride	look
im +	moral	mature	patient
	modest	pure	mortal
all +	most	ready	together
	though	so	one

SENTENCE LEVEL WORK

Grammar and punctuation

Subject and verb

> Every sentence has a *subject* – the person, place or thing the sentence is about.
>
> The rest of the sentence, including the verb, is called the *predicate*, eg
>
> 'Gregor Samsa awoke one morning.'
>   subject   predicate

A Copy these sentences. Underline the subject in one colour and the predicate in another colour.

1 He was transformed into a giant insect.

2 His legs were pitifully thin.

3 He felt a slight itching up on his belly.

4 The alarm-clock was ticking on the chest.

5 The next train went at seven o'clock.

B Copy the subject and the verb from each of these sentences.

1 He wouldn't avoid a row with the chief.

2 Gregor really felt quite well.

3 The porter was a creature of the chief's.

4 His mother tapped on the door.

5 He answered with a twittering squeak.

TEXT LEVEL WORK

Writing

Story openings

> The beginning of *Metamorphosis* is a very unusual *story opening*!
> It is unusual because:
> * the main character, Gregor, wakes up as a '*gigantic insect*'
> * he doesn't act in the way we would expect in this frightening situation!

Language features

Opening sentence

'*As Gregor Samsa awoke one morning from uneasy dreams he found himself transformed in his bed into a giant insect.*'

This opening sentence is designed to 'grab' the reader's attention so he/she will read on.

Writing in the third person
The narrator tells the story and does not appear in it, but he lets us know exactly what the main character is thinking.

Contrast
The writer describes Gregor's room, which is the setting of the story, in great detail. He does this because:
- it helps the reader understand that what is happening to Gregor is not a dream
- it is ordinary and unremarkable and provides a contrast to the remarkable thing which has happened to Gregor.

The writer introduces us to this weird and frightening situation and contrasts this with the ordinary thoughts and behaviour of the main character.

Writing assignment
Imagine that you found yourself in a similar situation to Gregor. You awake one morning and you have been transformed into something else!

Write the opening of your story. You could:
- use contrast: what has happened is extraordinary but you could think and act normally and describe a very normal setting
- think and act in a way that shows how frightened and confused you are and describe a 'nightmare' setting.

Remember:
- write in the first person: this is happening to you
- construct an attention-grabbing first sentence to make your reader want to read on
- describe your thoughts, feelings and surroundings carefully so the reader can imagine what you are going through and 'see' where you are.

Personal choice

Choose one of the following assignments.

1 Continue the story of Gregor Samsa and show:
- how he gets up and leaves his room
- how his mother reacts.

2 Write a paragraph to say why you would, or would not, like to read the rest of this story.

Later on

The novel traces the life of a horse called Black Beauty through a variety of adventures and mishaps. In this extract he is taking his master and mistress on a 46-mile journey to visit some friends. They have stopped overnight and the horses are in the stable of a large hotel.

Later on in the evening a traveller's horse was brought in by the second ostler, and whilst he was cleaning him, a young man with a pipe in his mouth lounged into the stable to gossip.

'I say, Towler,' said the ostler, 'just run up the ladder into the loft and put some hay down into this horse's rack, will you? Only lay down your pipe.'

'All right,' said the other, and went up through the trap door; and I heard him step across the floor overhead and put down the hay. James came in to look at us last thing and then the door was locked.

I cannot say how long I had slept, nor what time in the night it was, but I woke up very uncomfortable, though I hardly knew why. I got up; the air seemed all thick and choking. I heard Ginger coughing, and one of the other horses seemed very restless; it was quite dark, and I could see nothing, but the stable seemed very full of smoke, and I hardly knew how to breathe.

The trap door had been left open, and I thought that was the place it came through. I listened and heard a soft rushing sort of noise, and a low crackling and snapping. I did not know what it was, but there was something in the sound so strange that it made me tremble all over. The other horses were now all awake; some were pulling at their halters, others were stamping.

At last I heard steps outside, and the ostler who had put up the traveller's horse burst into the stable with a lantern, and began to untie the horses and try to lead them out; but he seemed in such a hurry, and so frightened himself that he frightened me still more. The first horse would not go with him; he tried the second and third, and they too would not stir. He came to me next and tried to drag me out of the stall by force; of course that was no use. He tried us all by turns and then left the stable.

No doubt we were very foolish, but danger seemed to be all around, and there was nobody we knew to trust in, and all was strange and uncertain. The fresh air that had come through the open door made it easier to breathe, but the rushing sound overhead grew louder, and as I looked upward, through the bars of my empty rack, I saw a red light flickering on the wall. Then I heard a cry of 'Fire' outside, and the old ostler quietly and quickly came in; he got one horse out, and went to another, but the flames were playing round the trap door, and the roaring overhead was dreadful.

The next thing I heard was James's voice, quiet and cheery, as it always was.

'Come, my beauties, it is time for us to be off, so wake up and come along.' I stood nearest the door, so he came to me first, patting me as he came in.

'Come, Beauty, on with your bridle, my boy; we'll soon be out of this smother.' It was on in no time; then he took the scarf off his neck, and tied it lightly over my eyes, and patting and coaxing he led me out of the stable. Safe in the yard, he slipped the scarf off my eyes, and shouted, 'Here, somebody! Take this horse while I go back for the other.'

A tall broad man stepped forward and took me, and James darted back into the stable. I set up a shrill whinny as I saw him go. Ginger told me afterwards that whinny was the best thing I could have done for her, for had she not heard me outside, she would never have had courage to come out.

There was much confusion in the yard; the horses being got out of other stables, and the carriages and gigs being pulled out of houses and shed, lest the flames should spread further. On the other side of the yard, windows were thrown up, and people were shouting all sorts of things; but I kept my eye fixed on the stable door, where the smoke poured out thicker than ever, and I could see flashes of red light; presently, I heard above all the stir and din, a loud clear voice, which I knew was master's.

'James Howard! James Howard! Are you there?' There was no answer but I heard a crash of something falling in the stable, and the next moment I gave a loud joyful neigh, for I saw James coming through the smoke, leading Ginger with him; she was coughing violently and he was not able to speak.

'My brave lad!' said master, laying his hand on his shoulder, 'Are you hurt?'

It's burning

The story is set in Australia and three boys, Harry, Wallace and Graham, have been allowed to go camping in the bush. One night, unable to sleep because of the wind and heat, Graham gets up to make coffee. He uses methylated spirits to start a fire and accidentally knocks over the bottle, which catches alight.

'It's *burning*' howled Graham.

A blue flame snaked from the little heater up through the rocks towards the bottle in the boy's hand; or at least that was how it seemed to happen. It happened so swiftly it may have deceived the eye. Instinctively, to protect himself, Graham threw the bottle away. There was a shower of fire from its neck, as from the nozzle of a hose.

'Oh my gosh,' yelled Wallace and tore off his sleeping-bag. 'Harry!' he screamed. 'Wake up, Harry!'

They tried to stamp on the fire, but their feet were bare and they couldn't find their shoes. They tried to smother it with their sleeping-bags, but it seemed to be everywhere. Harry couldn't even escape from his bag; he couldn't find the zip fastener, and for a few awful moments in his confusion between sleep and wakefulness he thought he was in his bed at home and the house had burst into flames around him. He couldn't come to grips with the situation; he knew only dismay and the wildest kind of alarm. Graham and Wallace, panicking, were throwing themselves from place to place, almost sobbing, beating futilely at a widening arc of fire. Every desperate blow they made seemed to fan the fire, to scatter it farther, to feed it.

'Put it out,' shouted Graham. 'Put it out.'

It wasn't dark any longer. It was a flickering world of tree trunks and twisted boughs, of scrub and saplings and stones, of shouts and wind and smoke and frantic fear. It was so quick. It was terrible.

'Put it out,' cried Graham, and Harry fought out of his sleeping-bag, knowing somehow that they'd never get it out by beating at it, that they'd have to get water up from the creek. But all they had was a four-pint billy-can.

The fire was getting away from them in all directions, crackling through the scrub down-wind, burning fiercely back into the wind. Even the ground was burning: grass, roots and fallen leaves were burning, humus was burning. There were flames on the trees, bark was burning, foliage was flaring, flaring like a whip-crack; and the heat was savage and searing and awful to breathe.

'We can't, we can't,' cried Wallace. 'What are we going to do?'

They beat at it and beat at it and beat at it.

'Oh gee,' sobbed Graham. He was crying, and he hadn't cried since he was twelve years old. 'What have I done? *We've got to get it out!*'

Harry was scrambling around wildly, bundling all their things together. It was not that he was more level-headed than the others; it was just that he could see the end more clearly, the hopelessness of it; the absolute certainty of it, the imminent danger of encirclement, the possibility that they might be burnt alive. He could see all this because he hadn't been in it at the start. He wasn't responsible; he hadn't done it; and now that he was wide awake he could see it more clearly. He screamed at them: 'Grab your stuff and run for it.' But they didn't hear him or didn't want to hear him. They were blackened, their feet were cut, even their hair was singed. They beat and beat, and the fire was leaping into the tree-tops, and there were no black shadows left, only bright light, red light, yellow light, light that was hard and cruel and terrifying, and there was a rushing sound, a roaring sound, explosions, and smoke, smoke like a red hot fog.

'No,' cried Graham. 'No, no, no.' His arms dropped to his sides and he shook with sobs and Wallace dragged him away. 'Oh, Wally,' he sobbed. 'What have I done?'

'We've got to get out of here,' shouted Harry. 'Grab the things and run.'

'Our shoes!' cried Wallace. 'Where are they?'

'I don't know. I don't know.'

'We've got to find our shoes.'

'They'll kill us.' sobbed Graham. 'They'll kill us. It's a terrible thing, an awful thing to have done.'

'Where'd we put our shoes?' Wallace was running around in circles, blindly. He didn't really know what he was doing. Everything had happened so quickly, so suddenly.

'For Pete's sake run!' shouted Harry.

Something in his voice seemed to get through to Wallace and Graham and they ran, the three of them, like frightened rabbits. They ran this way and that, hugging their packs and their scorched sleeping-bags, blundering into the scrub, even into the trunks of trees. Fire and confusion seemed to be all around them. The fire's rays darted through the bush; it was like an endless chain with a will of its own, encircling and entangling them, or like a wall that leapt out of the earth to block every fresh run they made for safety. Even the creek couldn't help them. They didn't know where it was. There might as well not have been a creek at all.

'This way,' shouted Harry, 'A track.'

They stumbled back down the track towards Tinley; at least they thought it was towards Tinley, they didn't really know. Perhaps they were running to save their lives, running simply from fear, running away from what they had done.

When they thought they were safe they hid in the bush close to a partly constructed house. They could hear sirens wailing; lights were coming on here and there; the head-lamps of cars were beaming and sweeping around curves in the track. They could hear shouts on the wind, they heard a woman cry hysterically, they heard Graham sobbing.

Over all was a red glow.

Ivan Southall

TEXT LEVEL WORK

Comprehension

A 1 What did Graham do to protect himself?

2 Why couldn't the boys stamp on the fire to put it out?

3 When Harry woke up and saw the fire, what at first did he think was happening?

4 Why couldn't the creek help them?

5 What evidence is there in the last paragraph that the fire has been seen by other people?

B 1 Why is Harry able to think more clearly than the other two boys?

2 What do you think Graham meant when he sobbed, '*They'll kill us*'.

3 What impression does the writer convey by using the simile '*they ran like frightened rabbits*'?

4 Find and copy three phrases describing the fire which:

- appeal to the sense of sight, ie what it looked like

- appeal to the sense of hearing, ie what it sounded like.

5 The writer describes the fire as almost human, having '*a will of its own*'. How does he create this impression?

C 1 How do you think the writer intended his readers to feel as they read this extract? Explain your reasons.

2 Explain in your own words how each of the characters reacts to the situation.

3 How does the final sentence in the chapter, '*Over all was a red glow*', make you feel?

WORD LEVEL WORK

Vocabulary

Dictionary work

Use a dictionary and the context of the extract to explain the meanings of these words.

1 instinctively
2 futilely
3 arc
4 frantic

5 foliage
6 searing
7 level-headed
8 imminent

9 singed
10 blundering
11 encircling
12 hysterically

Spelling

Homophones

Homophones are words which sound the same but have different spellings and meaning, eg

'A blue flame snaked from the little heater up **through** the rocks ...'
'Graham **threw** the bottle away.'

A Use each of these pairs of common homophones in one sentence to show you understand the different meanings.

1 there   their
2 see   sea
3 where   were
4 too   two
5 here   hear

6 hour   our
7 no   know
8 hole   whole
9 witch   which
10 for   four

B Write a homophone for each of these words. Use each pair of homophones in a sentence of your own.

1 saw
2 aloud
3 hare

4 rein
5 knight
6 pier

7 bred
8 creek
9 might

SENTENCE LEVEL WORK

Grammar and punctuation

Complex sentences

Remember:
- a simple sentence is made up of one main clause
- a compound sentence is made up of two or more simple sentences joined by a conjunction, eg

simple sentence: The fire was spreading.
simple sentence: They were afraid.
compound sentence: The fire was spreading and they were afraid.

A *complex sentence* is made up of one main clause and one or more other clauses called *subordinate clauses*. Subordinate clauses do not make sense on their own, eg

'Perhaps they were running to save their lives, running simply from fear, running away from what they had done.'

main clause: 'Perhaps they were running to save their lives'
subordinate clause: 'running simply from fear'
subordinate clause: 'running away from what they had done'

A 1 Copy these complex sentences and underline the main clause in each one.

1 Every desperate blow they made seemed to fan the fire, to scatter it, to feed it.

2 The fire was getting away from them in all directions, crackling through the scrub down-wind, burning fiercely in all directions.

3 Harry was scrambling around wildly, bundling all their things together.

4 They ran this way and that, hugging their packs and their scorched sleeping bags, blundering into the scrub, even into the trunks of trees.

5 When they thought they were safe they hid in the bush close to a partly constructed house.

TEXT LEVEL WORK

Writing

Complications and crises

The extract from *Ash Road* is a *crisis* point in the story that is very frightening for the characters involved. The writer successfully communicates their fear and panic to the reader by how he describes

- the situation getting worse and worse
- the reactions of the characters.

The crisis, although accidental, is brought on by the characters themselves through their carelessness.

Language features

Writing in the third person
This story is written in the third person, ie the narrator of the story is not one of the characters involved. In this way, the writer can tell us exactly how each of the characters is feeling in this dangerous situation and why they react as they do, eg

'to protect himself, Graham threw the bottle away.'
'he could see the end more clearly, the hopelessness of it'
'What have I done?'

Descriptive language
For the reader to feel the fear and panic experienced by the characters, the writer has to paint a vivid picture, using words, so that we can see the situation in our imagination. Compare these two descriptions:

'The wood was on fire.'

'There were flames on the trees, bark was burning, foliage was flaring, flaring like a whip-crack; and the heat was savage and searing and awful to breathe.'

Which description helps you to see the situation in your imagination?

Which description of the fire makes you feel as if you were actually there?

Imagine you were writing a story where the crisis point was a burst pipe and water was pouring through the ceiling. Improve this description:

'There was water coming through the ceiling.'

Dialogue

The characters' reaction to what is happening is shown through what they say. In a crisis, people do not usually just 'say' things. Here, the writer helps us to understand how the characters are feeling by using such words as 'howled' and 'yelled' instead of 'said'.

Re-read the extract and list the words the writer uses instead of 'said'.

Explain what difference it would have made if the writer had only used 'said'.

Resolution

The crisis in this extract from *Ash Road* is left as a 'cliffhanger'. This is the end of a chapter and we have to read on to find out how it will be resolved.

Writing assignment

In the third person, write the crisis point of a story which involves three characters. The situation is accidental but is brought on by one of the characters. In your planning you should:

> **HINT**
> You are not one of the characters in the story. You are the narrator.

* make notes about what has happened so far in the story

* decide on the characters involved in the crisis

* decide what the crisis is and how it is accidentally brought about

* list words and phrases you could use to paint a vivid picture of the situation

* decide on how each of the three characters responds to the crisis

* decide at what point to leave the crisis so that your reader will have to read on to find out how it is resolved.

Write your first draft

* using the third person

* organising this part of the story so that it ends on a 'high point' and the reader has to read on to find out how the crisis will be resolved.

Personal choice

Choose one of the following assignments.

1 Write an ending for the crisis in the extract from *Ash Road* based on what the writer has told us towards the end, ie

   * the boys were hiding in the bush close to a *'partly constructed house'*

   * they could hear sirens, shouts and a woman crying hysterically

   * they could see lights

   * Graham was sobbing.

2 Imagine that you had a dream about a fire in a forest and that the fire cannot harm you. Write a description in the first person of exactly what you see as you walk through the forest.

> **HINT**
> Writing in the first person means that it is happening to you. Use 'I' but do not begin every sentence with 'I'.

...a platform of forest

A group of boys of various ages has been stranded on an island after a plane crash. The only adult with them, the pilot, has not survived so the boys have to organise themselves and try to stay alive until help comes. One of their ideas is to light a big fire to attract passing ships or planes to their plight.

Below the other side of the mountain-top was a platform of forest. Once more Ralph found himself making the cupping gesture.

'Down there we could get as much wood as we want.'

Jack nodded and pulled at his underlip. Starting perhaps a hundred feet below them on the steeper side of the mountain, the patch might have been designed expressly for fuel. Trees forced by the damp heat, found too little soil for full growth, fell early and decayed: creepers cradled them, and new saplings searched a way up.

Jack turned to the choir, who stood ready. Their black caps of maintenance were slid over one ear like berets.

'We'll build a pile. Come on.'

They found the likeliest path down and began tugging at the dead wood. And the small boys who had reached the top came sliding too till everyone but Piggy was busy. Most of the wood was so rotten that when they pulled it broke up into a shower of fragments and woodlice and decay; but some trunks came out in one piece. The twins, Sam n' Eric, were the first to get a likely log but they could do nothing till Ralph, Jack, Simon, Roger and Maurice found room for a hand-hold. Then they inched the grotesque dead thing up the rock and toppled it over the top. Each party of boys added a quota, less or more, and the pile grew. At the return Ralph found himself alone on a limb with Jack and they grinned at each other, sharing this burden. Once more, amid the breeze, the shouting, the slanting sunlight on the high mountain, was shed that glamour, that strange invisible light of friendship, adventure, and content.

'Almost too heavy.'

Jack grinned back,

'Not for the two of us'

Together, joined in effort by the burden, they staggered up the last steep of the mountain. Together, they chanted One! Two! Three! and crashed the log on to the great pile. Then they stepped back, laughing with triumphant pleasure, so that immediately Ralph had to stand on his head. Below them, boys were still labouring, though some of the small ones had lost interest and were searching this new forest for fruit. Now the twins, with unsuspected intelligence, came up the mountain with armfuls of dried leaves and dumped them against the pile. One by one, as they sensed that the pile was complete the boys stopped going back for more and stood, with the pink, shattered top of the mountain around them. Breath came even by now, and sweat dried.

Ralph and Jack looked at each other while society paused about them. The shameful knowledge grew in them and they did not know how to begin confession.

Ralph spoke first, crimson in the face.

'Will you?'

He cleared his throat and went on.

'Will you light the fire?'

Now the absurd situation was open, Jack blushed too. He began to mutter vaguely.

'You rub two sticks. You rub –'

He glanced at Ralph, who blurted out the last confession of incompetence.

'Has anyone got any matches?'

William Golding

When midnight comes

Badger

When midnight comes a host of dogs and men
Go out and track the badger to his den,
And put a sack within the hole, and lie
Till the old grunting badger passes by.
He comes and hears – they let the strongest loose.
The old fox hears the noise and drops the goose.
The poacher shoots and hurries from the cry,
And the old hare half wounded buzzes by.
They get a forked stick to bear him down
And clap the dogs and take him to the town,
And bait him all the day with many dogs,
And laugh and shout and fright the scampering hogs.
He runs along and bites at all he meets:
They shout and hollo down the noisy streets.

He turns about to face the loud uproar
And drives the rebels to their very door.
The frequent stone is hurled where'er they go;
When badgers fight, then every one's a foe.
The dogs are clapped and urged to join the fray;
The badger turns and drives them all away.
Though scarcely half as big, demure and small
He fights with dogs for hours and beats them all.
The heavy mastiff, savage in the fray,
Lies down and licks his feet and turns away.
The bulldog knows his match and waxes cold.
The badger grins and never leaves his hold.
He drives the crowd and follows at their heels
And bites them through – the drunkard swears and reels.

The frighted women take the boys away,
The blackguard laughs and hurries on the fray.
He tries to reach the woods, an awkward race,
But sticks and cudgels quickly stop the chace.
He turns again and drives the noisy crowd
And beats the many dogs in noises loud.
He drives away and beats them every one,
And then they loose them all and set them on.
He falls as dead and kicked by boys and men,
Then starts and grins and drives the crowd agen;
Till kicked and torn and beaten out he lies
And leaves his hold and cackles, groans, and dies.

John Clare

Each morning

Each morning there were lambs with bloody mouth,

Their tongues cut out by foxes. Behind trees,

Where they had sheltered from the rainy South,

They'd rise to run, but fall on wobbly knees.

And knowing, though my heart was sick,

That only death could cure them of their ills,

I'd smash their heads in with handy stick

And curse the red marauders from the hills.

Each afternoon, safe in a sheltered nook

Behind the smithy, I'd prepare the bait;

And I remember how my fingers shook

With the half-frightened eagerness of hate

Placing the strychnine in the hidden rift

Made with the knife-point in the piece of liver;

And I would pray some fox would take my gift

And eat and feel the pinch and curse the giver.

Each night I'd lay abed sleepless until,

Above the steady patter of the rain,

I'd hear the first sharp yelp below the hill

And listen breathless till it rang again,

Nearer this time; then silence for a minute

While something in me waited for the leap

Of a wild cry with death and terror in it;

And then – it strikes me strange now – I could sleep.

Ernest G Moll

My mother saw a dancing bear

My mother saw a dancing bear
By the schoolyard, a day in June.
The keeper stood with chain and bar
And whistle-pipe, and played a tune.

And bruin lifted up its head
And lifted up its dusty feet,
And all the children laughed to see
It caper in the summer heat.

They watched as for the Queen it died.
They watched it march. They watched it halt.
They heard the keeper as he cried,
'Now, roly-poly!' 'Somersault!'

And then, my mother said, there came
The keeper with a begging-cup,
The bear with burning coat of fur,
Shaming the laughter to a stop.

They paid a penny for the dance,
But what they saw was not the show;
Only, in bruin's aching eyes,
Far-distant forests, and the snow.

Charles Causley

TEXT LEVEL WORK

Comprehension

A 1 Where was the poet's mother when she saw the dancing bear?

2 At what time of year did the dancing bear visit the town?

3 What musical instrument did the keeper play?

4 When the bear performed, what did it do?

5 What did the keeper do at the end of the bear's performance?

B 1 How did the keeper control the bear?

2 What does it mean when the poet says, 'They watched as for the Queen it died.'?

3 How much did the audience pay to see the bear perform?

4 What impression do you think the poet is trying to create when he says, 'The bear with burning coat of fur, Shaming the laughter to a stop.'?

5 What does the poet mean when he says, 'But what they saw was not the show; Only, in bruin's aching eyes, Far-distant forests, and the snow.'?

C 1 How did the poet's mother's feelings change during the time she watched the bear?

2 If you had been watching the bear

- what would have made you laugh?

- what would have impressed you about the bear?

- what would have saddened you?

WORD LEVEL WORK

Vocabulary

Dictionary work

Use a dictionary and the context of the poem to explain the meaning of these words.

1 schoolyard

2 whistle-pipe

3 bruin

4 caper

5 roly-poly

6 somersault

7 shaming

8 chain

9 bar

10 aching

11 begging-cup

12 keeper

Spelling

Unstressed vowels

> *Unstressed vowels* are vowels that we do not sound or do not sound very clearly as we speak. Unstressed vowels sometimes cause difficulties with spelling because we do not hear them clearly so we leave them out, eg
>
> **usually** 'Usually' sounds like 'usully' because the 'a' is an unstressed vowel.
>
> **interest** 'Interest' sounds like 'intrest' because the first 'e' is an unstressed vowel.

A Write the correct spellings of these words, putting in the unstressed vowels.

1 portrat
2 hygene
3 minral
4 proten
5 movment
6 reherse

7 litrature
8 vowl
9 estury
10 settlment
11 welth
12 wether

B Copy these words. Circle the unstressed vowels.

1 catholic
2 disease
3 parliament
4 priest
5 religious
6 siege

7 source
8 traitor
9 keyboard
10 spreadsheet
11 catalogue
12 dictionary

SENTENCE LEVEL WORK

Grammar and punctuation

Punctuating poetry

> The *use of capital letters and punctuation in poetry* is different from the way they are used in other types of writing. New lines usually begin with a capital letter. Often, lines end with a comma, to show that the reader should pause briefly, eg
>
> 'And bruin lifted up its head
> And lifted up its dusty feet,
> And all the children laughed to see
> It caper in the summer heat.

A Copy out the poem below, putting in capital letters and punctuation where you think they ought to go. Write a short explanation giving your reasons for punctuating as you have.

Bear

as a bear i am

capable of so

much running fast smearing honey

climbing trees and an apparent slow

thoughtfulness

it is hard then that i should only want

to be bear like really i

would swop it all any day to

live in highgate as a bad tempered old

grandfather person grumbling

kindly at children sore headed in

the garden growling when the

tea is late lumbering off

to play the piano in sulks in

a cold room in my heaviest overcoat

TEXT LEVEL WORK

Writing

Narrative poetry

Narrative poetry is poetry that tells stories of characters and events. In the poem *Mother Saw a Dancing Bear*, Charles Causley remembers a story told to him by his mother. She described to him an event from her own childhood and he wrote a poem about it.

However, the poet does not just tell a story, he also makes a point about the dancing bear. The dignity and grandeur of the bear shames the audience into silence. Although they pay for the show, the poet gives us the impression that the audience is sensing that the bear should be where he belongs. He should be living wild in the forests and the snows. We sense that the bear is remembering the wilderness, even though he is forced to dance for the audience.

Language features

Contrast

To make a point in a poem you can use contrast. You can start by setting the scene. Charles Causley describes

- his mother as being in the schoolyard, on a summer's day
- the performance of the bear
- the enjoyment of the audience.

However, in the last two verses, he changes the mood and our viewpoint – '*shaming the laughter to a stop*'. Finally, he encourages the reader to understand that the bear is a grand and dignified creature whose '*aching*' mind is still roaming the wildernesses of his home – '*Far-distant forests and the snow.*'

Writing assignment

Write a narrative poem from the viewpoint of the bear. Describe how he came to be a dancing bear and how he feels about it.

Try to create contrast in your poem by changing the mood towards the end.

Personal choice

Choose one of the following assignments.

1 Circuses and keepers of performing animals are sometimes criticised for cruelty to animals. Write your views on performing animals, giving reasons.

2 Imagine yourself as the poet's mother. Describe the day when you saw the dancing bear.

Then, from somewhere

The story is set in 1914 at the beginning of the First World War. Four young men, close friends from a Suffolk village who spend their time working in the fields and playing football, decide they will join the army and be part of the great 'adventure'. Life in the trenches in France is tough and they exist like 'bedraggled moles in a world of mud, attack and counter-attack'. Christmas brings the blessed relief of a cease-fire and a spontaneous game of football between the British and German army in No Man's Land.

Then, from somewhere, a football bounced across the frozen mud. Will was on it in a flash. He trapped the ball with his left foot, flipped it up with his right and headed it towards Freddie.

Freddie made a spectacular dive, caught the ball in both hands and threw it to a group of Germans.

Immediately a vast, fast and furious football match was under way. Goals were marked by caps. Freddie, of course, was in one goal and a huge German in the other.

Apart from that, it was wonderfully disorganised, part football, part ice-skating, with unknown numbers on each team. No referee, no account of the score.

It was just terrific to be no longer an army of moles, but up and running on top of the ground that had threatened to entomb them for so long. And this time Will really could hear a big crowd – and he was playing for England.

He was playing in his usual centre forward position with Lacey to his left and little Billy on the wing. The game surged back and forth across No Man's Land. The goalposts grew larger as greatcoats and tunics were discarded as the players warmed to the sport. Khaki and grey mixed together. Steam rose from their backs, and their faces were wreathed in smiles and clouds of breath in the clear frosty air. Some of the British officers took a dim view of such sport, and when the game came to its exhausted end, the men were encouraged back to their trenches for a carol service and supper. The haunting sound of men singing drifted back and forth across No Man's Land in the still night air.

'Good night, Tommies. See you tomorrow.'

'Good night, Fritz. We'll have another game.'

But Boxing Day passed without a game. The officers were alarmed at what had happened on Christmas Day. If such friendly relations continued, how could they get the men to fight again? How could the war continue?

The men were not allowed to leave the trenches. There were a few secret meetings here and there along the Front, and gifts and souvenirs were exchanged.

Two more days passed peacefully. Then a message was thrown over from the German side. A very important general was due to visit their section at 3.15 that afternoon and he would want to see some action. The Germans therefore would start firing at 3pm and the Tommies should please keep their heads down.

At three o'clock a few warning shots were fired over the British trenches and then heavy fire lasted for an hour. The Tommies kept their heads down.

At dawn a few days later, the Germans mounted a full-scale attack. The friendly Germans from Saxony had been withdrawn and replaced by fresh troops from Prussia. They were met by rapid and deadly fire from the British and were forced back.

The order was given to counter-attack, to try to take the German trenches before they could reorganise themselves. Will and the rest of the soldiers scrambled over the parapet.

Freddie still had the football! He drop-kicked it far into the mist of No Man's Land.

'That'll give someone a surprise,' he said.

'Why are goalies always daft?' thought Will.

They were on the attack. Running in a line, Will in a centre forward position, Lacey to his left, young Billy on the wing.

From the corner of his eye Will saw Freddie dive full-length, then curl up as if clutching a ball in the best goalkeeping tradition.

'Daft as a brush,' Will thought.

Suddenly they all seemed to be tackled at once. The whole line went down. Earth and sky turned over, and Will found himself in a shell hole staring at the sky. Then everything went black. Slowly the blackness cleared and Will could see the hazy sky once more. Bits of him felt hot and other bits felt very cold. He couldn't move his legs. He heard a slight movement. There was someone else in the shell hole.

Will dimly recognised the gleam of a fixed bayonet and the outline of a German.

'Wasser, Wasser,' the German said.

It was about the only German word Will knew. He fumbled for his water bottle and managed to push it towards the German with the butt of his rifle.

The German drank deeply. He didn't have the strength to return the bottle.

'*Kinder?*' he said. Will shook his head. The German held up three fingers. Will tried to shake his head again to show that he did not understand, but the blackness returned.

Later he saw a pale ball of gold in the misty sky. 'There's a ball in Heaven,' he thought. 'Thank God. We'll all have a game when this nightmare's over.'

At home when he had a bad dream he knew if he opened his eyes, the bad dream would end. But here, his eyes were already open.

Perhaps if he closed them, the nightmare would end.

He closed his eyes.

Michael Foreman

TEXT LEVEL WORK

Comprehension

A 1 In what two ways were the goals marked out?

2 The football match differed from a normal one in three ways. What were they?

3 What was going to happen at 3.15 that afternoon?

4 What first alerted Will that he was not alone in the shell hole?

5 What does the fact that Will gave his water bottle to the German soldier show you about him?

B 1 Both the troops from Prussia and the troops from Saxony mounted an attack on the British soldiers. In what way were the attacks different and why?

2 Explain the meaning of the following phrases in your own words:
a '*in a flash*'
b '*a dim view*'
c '*keep their heads down*'
d '*full-scale attack*'.

3 Will '*saw Freddie dive full-length, then curl up as if clutching a ball in the best goalkeeping tradition.*' His thoughts were, '*Daft as a brush.*' What do you think had really happened to Freddie?

4 What do you think the German was trying to ask Will when he said '*Kinder*'?

5 What evidence is there towards the end of the extract to show that Will is mixing up nightmare and reality?

C 1 As you read through the extract, how did your expectations of how it would end change? Write brief notes to show how you thought it might turn out at various points.

2 Do we know definitely what has happened to Will and the others at the end? What do you think will happen to them?

3 Why do you think the story is called '*War Game*'?

WORD LEVEL WORK

Vocabulary

Dictionary work

Use a dictionary and the context of the extract to explain the meanings of the following words.

1 spectacular	4 surged	7 exhausted	10 action
2 disorganised	5 discarded	8 haunting	11 mounted
3 entomb	6 wreathed	9 relations	12 parapet

Spelling

Plurals of words ending in y

> Remember, to make a noun plural we normally add 's', eg hand/hands
>
> If a noun ends in 's', 'x' 'ch' or 'sh', we add 'es', eg trench/trenches
>
> If a noun ends in 'o', we usually add 'es', eg hero/heroes
>
> If a noun ends in 'f' or 'fe', we usually change the 'f' or 'fe' to 'v' and add 'es', eg half/halves
>
> If a noun ends in 'y' we usually change the 'y' to 'i' and add 'es', eg army/armies
>
> If the letter before the 'y' is a vowel, we just add 's', eg day/days

A Write the plural for each of the words below.

1 technology	4 county	7 dictionary
2 frequency	5 estuary	8 glossary
3 laboratory	6 anthology	9 photocopy

B Write the plurals of these words.

1 football	4 wing	7 sound
2 ceremony	5 display	8 gift
3 match	6 calf	9 country

HINT

You will need to think about all the ways of forming plurals.

SENTENCE LEVEL WORK

Grammar and punctuation

Powerful verbs

> Verbs are very important types of words for a writer. Choosing *powerful verbs* helps to give the reader a vivid impression of the action, eg
>
> 'The game **surged** back and forth across No Man's Land. The goalposts **grew** larger as greatcoats and tunics **were discarded** as the players **warmed** to the sport. Khaki and grey **mixed** together. Steam **rose** from their backs, and their faces **were wreathed** in smiles and clouds of breath in the clear frosty air.'

Compare what the author wrote with this, where the powerful verbs have been replaced with weak, over-used ones.

'The game **went** back and forth across No Man's Land. The goalpost **got** larger as greatcoats and tunics **were taken** off as the players **got** into the sport. Khaki and grey **were** together. Steam **came** from their backs, and their faces **were covered** in smiles and clouds of breath in the clear frosty air.'

Which do you think gives a more vivid picture of the football match?

A Use a thesaurus and find three powerful verbs which are synonyms for each of these verbs.

1 got	4 saw	7 ran
2 said	5 asked	8 liked
3 took	6 ate	9 walked

> *HINT*
>
> A synonym means the same or nearly the same.

B Write five sentences, each one containing two of the powerful verbs you have found.

TEXT LEVEL WORK

Writing

Story endings

Deciding on a *story ending* is a very important part of planning the story. Not every story ends 'happily ever after'. In fact, the most effective story endings leave the reader with a variety of feelings.

In *War Game*, there is a 'cliffhanger' ending. The reader is left with many questions:

- Has Will died?
- Is he still alive but unconscious?
- Will he get out of the shell hole?
- What has happened to his friends?

The writer does not make it obvious how the story will end and readers will often have different ideas as to how the writer intended them to feel at the end.

Language features

Changing the reader's expectation

Throughout the extract, the dominant impression that the writer creates changes, making you unsure how it will all turn out.

1 The football game
'It was just terrific to be no longer an army of moles, but up and running on top of the ground that had threatened to entomb them for so long.'

The reader feels optimistic: the British and German soldiers have forgotten the war and are having a great time.
The ending: perhaps the story will end happily?

2 The officers' opinion
'*The officers were alarmed at what had happened on Christmas day. If such friendly relations continue, how could they get the men to fight again?*'

The reader is disturbed: will the officers stop them being friendly? Will the men refuse to fight?
The ending: a happy ending seems less certain.

3 The first German attack
'*Then a message was thrown over from the German side. A very important general was due to visit their section at 3.15 that afternoon and he wanted to see some action. The Germans therefore would start firing at 3pm and the Tommies should please keep their heads down.*'

The reader feels a sense of relief: the British soldiers have been warned about the 'attack'. The Germans are continuing the friendly relationship of the football match.
The ending: if the soldiers on both sides warn each other in this way, no one will be killed and it still could end happily.

4 The second German attack
'*At dawn a few days later, the Germans mounted a full-scale attack. The friendly Germans from Saxony had been withdrawn and replaced by fresh troops from Prussia. They were met by rapid and deadly fire from the British and were forced back.*'

The reader realises the situation has worsened: the football match is a dim memory.
The ending: the chances of a happy ending are very slim.

5 Over the parapet
'*Suddenly they all seemed to be tackled at once. The whole line went down and Will found himself in a shell hole staring at the sky. Then everything went black.*'

The reader feels hopeless: is anybody left alive?
The ending: it seems almost certain that Will is dead.

The cliffhanger ending
'*At home when he had a bad dream he knew if he opened his eyes, the bad dream would end. But here, his eyes were already open. / Perhaps if he closed them, the nightmare would end. / He closed his eyes.*'

Is the reader sure Will is dead? If he is still alive will he be rescued? Will he be captured?

Writing assignment
Write a short story with a cliffhanger ending. It should have no more than three characters and can be based on one of the titles below, or you can use your own ideas.

- 'It Wouldn't Have Happened If ...'
- 'The Accident'
- 'All in a Day's Work'

Personal choice

Choose one of these assignments.
1 Imagine this is not the ending to *War Game* but a crisis. Write a resolution for the crisis.
2 Imagine you are Will and are lying, injured, in the shell hole. It is many hours before you are rescued. Write the thoughts that go through your mind as you lie in the darkness.

'Soldiers, today you will

This short story is told from the point of view of the Mission Commander. Early on in the story he speaks to his men before they are to go into battle.

'Soldiers, today you will make history that your children will read. Your children's children, perhaps, will remember your part in the history of our great nation. Free men will always be called upon to make sacrifices that freedom may survive. Some of my senior soldiers will remember other battles in Germany, France and North Africa, where their comrades died in order that the younger men among you could grow up in freedom. Now, you in turn are to be asked to do the same. We will prove true to that trust in us.' It was going well, damned well. I had their attention; they had even to some extent forgotten the cold. 'You are a part of the finest, best-equipped and most scientific army that the world has ever seen. We were not sent here to fight, but we brought weapons with us because the Government knew that these people who use the word "peace" so often, who profess to bring brotherhood and prosperity to the whole world, have nothing but hatred and envy in their hearts.'

The men are sent off to break camp and prepare to march. The Mission Commander is talking to his second in command when ...

The scream cut through the air like a spurt of blood. Three of our men, their uniforms mud-splattered and torn, were running as fast as Olympic champions. Behind them there was a fourth. He was holding his side as he ran, leaving a trail of red spots, each one bigger than the last. The whole unit broke formation as the three men of the advance party ran past them without even a glance at their comrades. The fourth man was level with me now, and I stepped out to stand in his path. He stopped. His eyes were huge and full of tears. 'You said they were men!' he accused. 'You said we'd be fighting men!' His voice was shrill to the point of hysteria. His helmet was askew, but the spider of blood on his jaw told me that it was the boy I'd spoken with. I grabbed his arm but he broke away from me with a surprising force. I looked down and found that my tunic was smeared with fresh shiny blood from the youngster's wounds. I watched him as he followed the others down a steep incline, dodging between the rocky outcrops. 'Come back!' I shouted. The wind snatched my voice away. I cupped my hands round my mouth, 'Come back at once! I'll have you executed!'

It was no use. The rest of them had sniffed the scent of panic and were scrambling down the hillside too. Only a few of the hardiest old campaigners remained in the roadway looking the way the four men had come. For a moment I had hope, but then they saw the sight that the others had seen and they too gibbered with fear.

'Don't be afraid,' I said, 'don't be afraid. I've seen them before. They are large, but they are controlled by men no better than us.'

Two of my senior sergeants then prostrated themselves on the roadway, screaming a mixture of prayers and oaths that betrayed a mankind for whom witchcraft lay just under the skin of science.

Other soldiers were ripping their hands and legs on the rocks and stony ledges below me as they half-ran and half-fell towards the sheltered basin in which we had camped the previous night, 'Alive!' my soldiers were shouting. 'They are alive! They are alive!'

They would not escape. There was no escape from here. Already some of the men who had fallen were not able to regain their feet. A thousand feet below me were men who could have got there only by throwing themselves bodily from the narrow crevasse. Wearily, I turned back to where my second-in-command was standing. He'd not moved.

'Who could have believed it?' I asked, as I stood there with the bald officer: just two of us between the invaders and the rich, lush land of Italy. 'Who could have believed that Hannibal would bring elephants over the Alps?'

Len Deighton

TEXT LEVEL WORK

Comprehension

A 1 Who is addressing the soldiers in the opening speech?

 2 Why have the army brought weapons with them?

 3 How do we know that the '*fourth man*' is wounded?

 4 When the soldiers had '*sniffed the scent of panic*', what do they do?

 5 Why is there '*no escape*' from the position the army is in?

B 1 What do you think the Commander means when he says, '*It was going well*'?

 2 He says '*We were not sent here to fight*'. What do you think the army was sent there for?

 3 What effect is the writer trying to make when uses the simile '*like a spurt of blood*' to describe the scream?

 4 Explain in your own words what the writer means by '*a mankind for whom witchcraft lay just under the skin of science*'.

 5 What evidence in the text is there to show that the soldiers had not seen elephants before?

C 1 After the Commander's speech, what impression are you left with about the ending of the story?

 2 When the fourth man shouts, '*You said we'd be fighting men!*', what thoughts did you have about what he had seen?

 3 In what way was the ending to the story a surprise?

WORD LEVEL WORK

Vocabulary

Dictionary work

Use a dictionary and the context of the story to explain the meanings of these words:

1 sacrifices	5 comrades	9 gibbered
2 prosperity	6 hysteria	10 prostrated
3 spurt	7 askew	11 crevasse
4 formation	8 hardiest	12 lush

Spelling

Suffixes ous and ious

The suffixes *ous* and *ious* can confuse even good spellers!
Sometimes you can't hear the 'i' and the word sounds just like an 'ous' ending, eg

 enorm**ous**   feroc**ious**

Sometimes you can hear the 'i', eg

 ser**ious**   victor**ious**

A Copy and finish the answers to the clues by adding 'ous' or 'ious'.

	Clue	Answer
1	wonderful	marvell_____
2	tasty	delic_____
3	giving freely	gener_____
4	playing tricks	mischiev_____
5	solemn	ser_____
6	bad tempered and spiteful	vic_____
7	savage, wildly cruel	feroc_____
8	happened before	prev_____
9	having a religion	relig_____
10	being the winner	victor_____

> **HINT**
>
> Use a dictionary to check your spelling.

B Learn to spell the words you have formed in **A** along with these important 'ous' and 'ious' words.

conscious	continuous	jealous
miscellaneous	nervous	outrageous

> To add 'ous' or 'ious' to most words ending in 'our' omit the 'u' in the root word, eg
>
> vigour   vigor**ous**

C Add 'ous' or 'ious' to these root words and use each one in a sentence of your own.

1 vapour   2 humour   3 labour   4 glamour

SENTENCE LEVEL WORK

Grammar and punctuation

Direct speech

> We use *speech marks* ' ' at the beginning and end of the words that a person actually said, including the sentence punctuation, eg
>
> "Come back at once!"
>
> opening speech mark   closing speech mark
>
> spoken words   sentence punctuation
>
> When a different person speaks, we begin a new paragraph, eg
>
> "What have you seen?" asked the soldier as he stared fearfully across the mountains.
>
> "They're huge! They're alive!" screamed the wounded man.

A Copy and punctuate these direct-speech sentences.

1 You will do your duty ordered the Commander.

2 Run screamed the wounded soldier.

3 Stand and fight bellowed the Commander.

4 What are they asked the second-in-command

5 Who would have believed it he said.

> **HINT**
>
> Speech marks are sometimes called inverted commas.

B Copy the conversation and add the correct punctuation. Remember the rule when a different person speaks.

HINT

Remember the punctuation before the final speech marks.

What sort of weapons do you think they will bring with them asked Marcus. I don't know replied Gaius. Have you ever seen Hannibal's army before queried Marcus. I've heard about it but I have never seen it, said Gaius.

Sometimes the *spoken words are split*.
If the spoken words are one sentence, we put a comma before the first closing speech mark and after such words as said, shouted, asked etc, eg

"Come back at once," he screamed, "or I'll have you executed!"

first part of the sentence   second part of the sentence

comma   comma

If the spoken words are two sentences, we put a full stop, exclamation mark or question mark before the first closing speech mark and a full stop after said, shouted, asked etc, eg

"Come back!" I shouted. "Come back at once!"

first speech sentence   second speech sentence

exclamation mark   full stop

C Copy and punctuate the split speech.

1 We have brought our weapons explained the Commander because we do not trust them

2 I've never seen elephants before said the soldier I wonder what they look like

3 If you ask me said Marcus it's a lot of fuss about nothing

4 You wouldn't be saying that if you'd fought elephants warned the second-in command You just wait

5 Who would have believed sighed the Commander that Hannibal would bring his elephants across the Alps.

TEXT LEVEL WORK

Writing

Story endings

Writers try to make sure that their readers cannot guess the *story ending*. Even if everything turns out fine in the end, a writer often disguises this to keep the reader guessing.

Sometimes a writer can make you think one thing is happening throughout the story and it is not until you reach the end that you find out how mistaken you were. The ending takes you by surprise.

Here, the writer makes us believe we are reading about a modern army so it is quite a surprise to find out that we are reading about Hannibal's campaign against the Romans in 216BC!

Language features

Disguise

The writer of *Mission Control: Hannibal One* disguises the true nature of the army by his choice of words in the Commander's speech. These have a very modern feel to them, eg

Mission Control   comrades   scientific

We feel that this is a modern army on a peace-keeping mission.

Vocabulary choices

The writer is careful to choose words that will not 'give the game away', eg

uniforms   unit   advance party   helmet

All these words could be used in almost any war story, no matter what period in history.

Clues

Once the writer has convinced us that we are reading about a modern army, he puts in clues to puzzle us, eg

The wounded soldier shouts, *"You said we'd be fighting men!"*

Immediately we begin to wonder what he has seen and probably think it is some kind of fighter bomber or tank.

When the soldiers begin to shout, *"Alive ...They are alive!"* we are really puzzled.

The surprise ending

The writer leaves us guessing until the very end:

'Who could have believed it? ... Who could have believed that Hannibal would bring elephants over the Alps?'

Writing assignment

Write a short story with a surprise ending. It should have no more than three characters and can be based on the titles below, or you can use your own ideas:

- My First Day
- A Tricky Situation
- Discovery!

Remember to:

- disguise what is really going on in your story
- surprise the reader at the very end.

Personal choice

Choose one of the following assignments.

1 Write a narrative poem about the sighting of the elephants as Hannibal appeared to the waiting Roman army.

2 Imagine you are one of the advance party who sees Hannibal and his army and watches them as the elephants approach. Write a vivid description of:

- what they look like
- what they sound like
- how they move.

...as I emerged

In H G Wells's novel The War of the Worlds *the Martians invade Earth. On seeing them for the first time, the narrator describes them as 'a big greyish, rounded bulk, the size perhaps of a bear'. The Martians build huge machines in which to move around. People flee in terror as the Martians begin to take over the Earth with a cloying Red Weed and kill all in their sight. Plans are made and weapons used to overcome them but nothing works. Towards the end of the novel, the narrator is making his way through London alone, 'intensely weary, footsore, and now and again hungry and thirsty', the only sound a strange 'Ulla, ulla, ulla' ringing out across the deserted city.*

... as I emerged from the top of Baker Street, I saw far away over the trees in the clearness of the sunset the hood of the Martian giant from which this howling proceeded. I was not terrified. I came upon him as if it were a matter of course. I watched him for some time, but he did not move. He appeared to be standing and yelling for no reason I could discover ...

I came upon the wrecked Handling Machine half-way to St John's Wood

Station. At first I thought a house had fallen across the road. It was only as I clambered among the ruins that I saw, with a start, this mechanical Samson lying, with its tentacles bent and smashed and twisted, among the ruins it had made. The forepart was shattered. It seemed as if it had driven blindly straight at the house, and had been overwhelmed by its overthrow ...

Wondering still more at all that I had seen, I pushed on towards Primrose Hill. Far away, through the gap in the trees I saw a second Martian, motionless as the first, standing in the park towards the Zoological Gardens, and silent. A little beyond the ruins about the smashed Handling Machine I came upon the Red Weed again, and found Regent's Canal a spongy mass of dark-red vegetation.

Abruptly, as I crossed the bridge, the sound of 'Ulla, ulla, ulla,' ceased. It was, as it were, cut off. The silence came like a thunder-clap.

The dusky houses about me stood faint and tall and dim; the trees towards the park were growing black. All about me the Red Weed clambered among the ruins, writhing to get above me in the dim. Night, the Mother of Fear and Mystery, was coming upon me. But while that voice sounded, the solitude, the desolation, had been endurable; by virtue of it London had still seemed alive, and the sense of life about me had upheld me. Then suddenly a change, the passing of something – I knew not what – and then a stillness that could be felt. Nothing but this gaunt quiet.

London about me gazed at me spectrally. The windows in the white houses were like the eye-sockets of skulls. About me my imagination found a thousand noiseless enemies moving. Terror seized me, a horror of my temerity. In front of me the road became pitchy black as though it was tarred and I saw a contorted shape lying across the pathway. I could not bring myself to go on. I turned down St John's Wood Road, and ran headlong from this unendurable stillness towards Kilburn. I hid from the night and the silence, until long after midnight, in a cabmen's shelter in the Harrow Road. But before the dawn my courage returned, and while stars were still in the sky, I turned once more towards Regent's Park. I missed my way among the streets, and presently saw, down a long avenue, in the half-light of the early dawn, the curve of Primrose Hill. On the summit, towering up to the fading stars, was a third Martian, erect and motionless like the others.

An insane resolve possessed me. I would die and end it. And I would save myself even the trouble of killing myself. I marched on recklessly towards this Titan, and then, as I drew nearer and the light grew, I saw that a multitude of black birds was circling and clustering about the hood. At that my heart gave a bound, and I began running along the road.

I hurried through the Red Weed that choked St Edmund's Terrace (I waded breast-high across a torrent of water that was rushing down from the water-works towards the Albert Road), and emerged upon the grass before the rising of the sun. Great mounds had been heaped about the crest of the hill, making a huge redoubt of it – it was the final and largest place the Martians made – and from behind these heaps there rose a thin smoke against the sky.

Against the skyline an eager dog ran and disappeared. The thought that had flashed into my mind grew real, grew credible. I felt no fear, only a wild trembling exultation, as I ran up the hill towards the motionless monster. Out of the hood hung lank shreds of brown at which the hungry birds pecked and tore.

In another moment I had scrambled up the earthen rampart and stood upon its crest, and the interior of the redoubt was below me. A mighty space it was, with gigantic machines here and there within it, huge mounds of material and strange shelter-places. And, scattered about it, some in their over-turned war-machines, some in now rigid Handling Machines, and a dozen of them stark and silent and laid in a row, were the Martians – *dead!* – slain by the putrefactive and disease bacteria against which their systems were unprepared; slain as the Red Weed was being slain; slain, after all man's devices had failed, by the humblest things that God, in His wisdom, has put upon this earth.

H G Wells

TEXT LEVEL WORK

Comprehension

A 1 What part of the Martian does the narrator see as he emerged *'from the top of Baker Street'*?

2 What is it doing?

3 With what does the narrator compare the windows in the white houses? How does this make him feel?

4 What was the narrator's *'insane resolve'*?

5 What has killed the Martians?

B 1 Why do you think the narrator is *'not terrified'* when he sees the Martian?

2 What do you think the narrator means when he calls the Handling Machine a *'mechanical Samson'*?

3 Explain in your own words how the narrator feels when the *'Ulla, ulla, ulla'* sound stops abruptly.

4 Explain in your own words:
a *'Night, the Mother of Fear and Mystery'*
b *'a contorted shape'*
c *'marched on recklessly'*.

5 The narrator says, *'The thought that had flashed into my mind grew real, grew credible'*. What *'thought'* do you think he had?

C 1 Make a list of the words and phrases in the extract which lead the reader to the conclusion that something is wrong with the Martians.

2 Were you prepared for the ending or were you surprised? Explain your reasons.

WORD LEVEL WORK

Vocabulary

Dictionary work

Use a dictionary and the context of the story to explain the meanings of these words.

1 emerged	4 endurable	7 resolve	10 exultation
2 motionless	5 temerity	8 redoubt	11 putrefactive
3 writhing	6 contorted	9 credible	12 devices

Spelling

Suffixes able and ible

Many words have the suffix *able* or *ible*, eg

endur**able**   cred**ible**

It is not easy to decide when to use 'able' and when to use 'ible'.

- if the antonym of the word is made by adding the prefix 'un', it is probably an 'able' word, eg

  endur**able**   **un**endur**able**

- if the antonym of the word is not formed with 'un' it is probably an 'ible' word, eg

  cred**ible**   **in**cred**ible**

HINT

About five times more words end in 'able' than 'ible'.

A Copy and complete the words below by adding 'able' or 'ible'.

1 unsuit_____
2 invis_____
3 unus_____
4 unreason_____
5 insens_____

6 irrespons_____
7 unbeliev_____
8 illeg_____
9 unlov_____

HINT

Remember, when adding a suffix that begins with a vowel to a word that ends with 'e', we normally drop the 'e'.

B As with all rules there are exceptions. These words do not follow the guidelines about prefixes. You need to learn them!

intolerable	inseparable	incurable	indescribable
improbable	dishonourable	incapable	disagreeable

SENTENCE LEVEL WORK

Grammar and punctuation

Conditional sentences

A *conditional sentence* is one where one action depends upon another, eg

'The Martians might take over the whole planet unless we can stop them.'

'unless we can stop them' = conditional clause

The Martians taking over the planet depends on whether or not we can stop them.

'The Martians will all die if they continue to eat and drink.'

'if they continue to eat and drink' = conditional clause

All the Martians dying depends on whether or not they continue to eat and drink.

A Copy and complete these conditional sentences.

1 The Handling Machine might have moved if _____.
2 He would cross the bridge if _____.
3 He might be terrified if _____.
4 The Red Weed would continue to spread unless _____.
5 I thought all the Martians were dead unless _____.

B Copy and complete these conditional sentences by adding a main clause.

1 _____ if I made my way to Primrose Hill.
2 _____ if the Martian saw me.
3 _____ unless I could hide in the cabmen's shelter.
4 _____ if I couldn't find anyone else left alive.
5 _____ if the Martians were dead.

> If the *conditional clause* comes first in the sentence, it is separated from the main clause by a comma, eg
>
> 'If I walked up to the Martian, it would surely kill me.'
>
> conditional clause   comma   main clause

C Use these conditional clauses in sentences of your own.

(if I can escape from England)   (if Martians invaded the earth)

(unless I know where to go)

(if what I believe is true)

(unless the Martians are stopped)

HINT
Use some of the conditional clauses at the beginning of the sentence. Remember the comma.

TEXT LEVEL WORK

Writing

Story endings

> A writer will sometimes prepare the reader for the *story ending* by giving clues as to how things might turn out.
>
> In the ending to *The War of the Worlds*, H G Wells builds up the impression that all is not well with the Martians.
>
> At the same time he keeps the readers guessing because we have no idea what has happened to make the Martians motionless.

Language features

Writing in the first person

Writing in the first person means that you can only tell the reader as much as you know.

- We discover things at the same time as the narrator:
  'the sound of the "Ulla, ulla, ulla," ceased. It was, as it were, cut off.'
  The narrator can only describe the noise ceasing. He does not know the reason so the readers do not.

- We see what the narrator sees:
  'On the summit... was a third Martian, erect and motionless like the others.'
  The narrator does not know why the Martian is *'motionless'* and so we do not.

Building tension

The writer wants us to see and feel everything the narrator is going through so we experience the tension of the situation.

- We see: the hood of the Martian giant; the wrecked Handling Machine; a spongy mass of dark red vegetation; a contorted shape
- We feel: the solitude, the desolation; the terror; unendurable stillness.

We understand his *'insane resolve'* to kill himself.

Changing the mood

Up to this point the dominant impression has been one of fear and despair. Now the writer changes the mood. We discover:

- *'a multitude of black birds was circling and clustering around the hood'*
- *'over-turned war-machines'*
- *'now rigid Handling Machines'*
- *'a dozen of them stark and silent and laid in a row, were the Martians – dead!'*

We can understand why:

- *'my heart gave a bound'*
- *'The thought that had flashed into my mind grew real, grew credible.'*
- *'I felt no fear, only a wild trembling exultation'*.

The surprise ending

The writer had laid the clues for us to follow so we know that everything is going to turn out well but he still has a surprise in store. The Martians have been *'slain, after all man's devices had failed, by the humblest things that God, in His wisdom, has put upon this earth'*.

Writing assignment

Write a short story where the reader is given clues as to how it will end.

- Write in the first person so you can only let your readers know and see as much as you, as the narrator, know and see.

- Change the mood so your readers think either that the story is going to end badly (build the tension) but it actually turns out well (give the reader clues)

or

it is going to end well (the dominant impression is that everything is going well) but it actually turns out badly (give the reader clues).

Personal choice

Choose one of the following assignments.

1 Imagine that when the narrator hides in the cabmen's shelter, he discovers another person who is still alive and fleeing the Martians. Write their conversation.

2 Write the opening two paragraphs of your own story about the Martians coming to earth.

Scene: A living-room

Part One

Characters:

Mother   Father   Stephen   Linda

Scene: A living-room

MOTHER   Stephen? Come on, it's dinner time!

STEPHEN   What are we eating?

LINDA   Pork!

MOTHER   Pork chops.

STEPHEN   I don't want any.

MOTHER   What do you mean?

LINDA   It's your favourite, you're always asking for it.

STEPHEN   I just don't want any. I'd like an egg. Two eggs. I'll do them myself.

MOTHER   No you won't young man. Those are for breakfast. If you go on like this I'll be cross. Dad'll be home soon and I want the rest of you out of the way. He's had a long day and he wants to have his dinner in peace.

LINDA (*sitting down*) Well, I'm not waiting.

MOTHER (*sitting down too*) You can join us or not as you please but leave the eggs alone.

STEPHEN (*still not sitting down*) I'm a vegetarian.

MOTHER   What?

STEPHEN   A vegetarian.

LINDA   Hark at him, he must have gone religious.

STEPHEN   No I haven't. I just don't eat meat.

MOTHER   Stephen, for heaven's sake, why?

STEPHEN   It's wrong.

LINDA   But you do eat meat. You've eaten it every day for fourteen years.

STEPHEN   And now I've stopped.

MOTHER   What, just like that?

STEPHEN   Yes. I think it's immoral.

MOTHER   Stephen, if this is your idea of a joke it's gone far enough. Your chops will go cold with all this fooling about.

STEPHEN   But I'm serious. I mean what I say.

LINDA   Don't worry Mum, it's only a phase. It'll be something else next week. You know what he's like.

STEPHEN (*shouting*) I mean what I say!

MOTHER   Well, after all we've done for you. Here's your father, look, for the last time ... (*Stephen shakes his head*)

MOTHER (*furious*) I didn't buy this expensive food for you to waste it!

FATHER (*coming in*) Hey, what's going on? What's he been doing, what have you done, my lad?

STEPHEN   Nothing Dad.

LINDA   Dad, he's had a religious conversion!

MOTHER   He says he's a vegetarian. He won't eat meat.

FATHER (*amused*) Well, that's his funeral, isn't it? He'll soon get hungry. Anyway, I'm hungry, and whatever you've made it smells good.

MOTHER   Sit down darling, I'll dish it up.

FATHER   Thanks, mm, very good (*taking a big forkful*). Excellent. (*Stephen is standing stubbornly with his arms folded*) Who put you up to this? You're no vegetarian, you're a carnivore through and through. Whose idea was it?

STEPHEN   My idea. I've been thinking.

LINDA   Hark at him! What next?

STEPHEN   Animals have as much right to live as we do.

FATHER   Rights? What do you know about rights? In this life you get what you get. This sheep probably got more out of life than you do.

STEPHEN   We killed it. Anyway it's not a sheep, it's a pig.

LINDA   Was a pig. Dirty things ...

STEPHEN   Pigs are famous for being affectionate.

LINDA   Mum, I know what it is! It's that film about the pig he saw last week, the pig that got stolen and everybody wanted to eat! It sounded stupid to me!

STEPHEN Why don't you shut up, you don't understand anything. (*To his parents*) It was a serious film, about serious ideas. It was funny on the surface, but sad underneath.

FATHER What do you wear on your feet, Steve?

STEPHEN Shoes.

FATHER And what are they made of?

STEPHEN OK, leather. I get the point.

FATHER What's your wallet made of?

LINDA Pigskin!

STEPHEN Shut up, you!

FATHER Is that a leather belt I see?

STEPHEN All right, you've made your point! (*he's angry*) I can't change everything overnight.

LINDA Dad, he says he wants to eat eggs, but eggs are baby chicks!

STEPHEN They're not, you little ... (*tries to slap her but is restrained by his father*)

FATHER No you don't! You lay a finger on Linda and you'll be sorry!

STEPHEN She's just trying to wind me up. You all are. Well I'm not sticking around here. I'm off!

Michael Church and Betty Tadman

TEXT LEVEL WORK

Comprehension

A 1 What is the family eating?

2 How old is Stephen?

3 Why does Linda say that Stephen has had '*a religious conversion*'?

4 What does Stephen's Father mean when he says, '*You're a carnivore through and through*'?

5 Why does Stephen's Father mention his '*shoes*', '*wallet*' and '*belt*'?

B 1 What is Stephen's Mother's attitude to his change of diet?

2 How does Linda react to Stephen's decision to be a vegetarian?

3 Does Stephen's Father take his decision to be a vegetarian seriously, at first?

4 Does Stephen's Father's attitude change as the scene progresses?

5 How does Stephen feel about his family's reactions to his decision?

C 1 What arguments can you find in the extract for and against eating meat?

2 Stephen says, '*Animals have as much right to live as we do.*' What are your views?

WORD LEVEL WORK

Vocabulary

Dictionary work

Use a dictionary and the context of the play to explain the meaning of the following words. Use each word in a sentence of your own, so that the meaning is clear.

1 chops	4 conversion	7 funeral	10 restrained
2 vegetarian	5 immoral	8 carnivore	11 expensive
3 religious	6 phase	9 affectionate	12 amused

Spelling

Suffix ful

> Adding the suffix *ful* to a word makes it into an adjective, eg
>   peace + **ful** = peaceful
> Peaceful means 'full of peace'.

A Add the suffix 'ful' to each word then use that word in a sentence of your own.

1 force	4 fear	7 hate	10 sorrow
2 care	5 dread	8 joy	11 worship
3 hope	6 awe	9 disgrace	12 thought

> Remember. If a word ends in 'y', you usually need to change
> the 'y' to an 'i' before adding a suffix, eg
>   beau**ty** + ful = beautiful

B Use the suffix 'ful' to change each of the following words into an adjective.

1 fancy	3 plenty	5 play
2 mercy	4 duty	6 pity

SENTENCE LEVEL WORK

Grammar and punctuation

Active and passive voice

> Remember, in English sentences the subject carries out the action
> (verb) and the object is the receiver of the action, eg
>   Stephen disliked meat.
>   subject verb object
> This gives the basic pattern for English sentences: subject + verb + object.
> This arrangement is called the *active voice*.
>
> The arrangement of English sentences varies, so it is possible for the
> basic pattern of an English sentence to be changed, eg
>   Meat is disliked by Stephen.
>   object verb   subject
> Here, the pattern of the sentence has been changed from:
> subject + verb + object   to   object + verb + subject.
> Now the receiver of the action is put first and the subject who
> carries out the action is put last.
> This arrangement is called the *passive voice*.

The active voice tends to be simple, clear and direct.
The active voice also produces more interesting and forceful writing.
A sentence is more effective when it focuses on the subject that is doing something, instead of a subject that is being acted upon.

A Copy the table below. Identify the active and passive voice for each sentence. Don't forget to look for the subject who is acting upon the object:

- subject first/object last = active voice
- object first/subject last = passive voice.

HINT

Do not change from active to passive in the same sentence.

Sentence	Voice
1 Stephen changed his beliefs.	
2 Linda mocked Stephen.	
3 Linda was attacked by Stephen.	
4 Stephen was restrained by his Father.	
5 Stephen ran out of the room.	

TEXT LEVEL WORK

Writing

Playscripts

Playscripts are written to record *dialogue* (speech) between the characters who act out the play. The name of each character is written at the left of the script, to show who is speaking each line.

A script also include *stage directions* for the director, stage crew and actors, to suggest how the scene should be played.

Plays are often divided into sections, called *acts*. Acts are often divided into shorter sections, called *scenes*. Sometimes, scenes have the lines numbered, so that it is quick and easy to find your place in the script.

At the start of each act or scene, the script usually tells you where the action is taking place.

Language features

Setting the scene
At the beginning of each act or scene, the playwright explains where the action is taking place, eg

A living-room

Dialogue
The language of a playscript imitates speech, even though it is in written form. It will have

- pauses   'Thanks, mm, very good (*taking a big forkful*). Excellent.'
- incomplete sentences   'They're not, you little ...'
- one-word sentences   'Pigskin!'

Through the dialogue in a play the audience finds out about the characters.

Stage directions

These help the actors and actresses:

- to know what tone of voice the line should be said in, eg

  shouting   furious   amused

- to know what gestures and actions to make, eg

  Stephen shakes his head.   tries to slap her but is restrained by his father.

Writing assignment

Write Scene 2 of *Animal Rights*. In your planning you must decide:

• where the scene takes place:	Will it be in the living-room as in Scene 1, somewhere else in the house, or away from the house?
• when the scene takes place:	Is it the same evening, the next day or later?
• what characters will be in the scene:	Will you include all four of the characters in Scene 1 or only some of them? Will you introduce a new character?
• who is the main character:	Is it Stephen, as in Scene 1, or does one of the other characters take the lead?
• what does this character want:	If it is Stephen, he wants to be allowed to be a vegetarian. If it is one of the other characters, does he/she want to persuade Stephen not to be a vegetarian or does Stephen convince him/her that his views are right?
• how does this character put his/her ideas across:	Is he/she calm, angry, confused?
• what do the other characters in the scene add to what is going on:	Do they agree, disagree, try to put forward a compromise?
• what does the main character do to get what he/she wants:	Is he/she reasonable, awkward, determined?
• does the main character succeed or fail to get what he/she wants:	?

Set your playscript out in the same way as *Animal Rights* Part One:

- the names of the characters on the left
- the dialogue in one colour
- the stage directions in another colour and in brackets.

If you are using a word processor, you can use different fonts instead of colours.

Personal choice

Choose one of the following assignments.

1. Imagine you are Stephen. Write a diary entry about what has just happened in the living-room.
2. Write a description of Stephen and the other characters in his family. Remember to use a wide range of adjectives and figures of speech (eg, metaphors and similes). You could draw the characters and their costumes to illustrate your descriptions.

Where is the party?

The action of the play takes place in a short stretch of back-alley (known as a 'ten-foot') behind a block of houses. The play concerns the comings and goings of the children who live in the houses along the road. They tend to gather around the lamp-post outside No. 23 and we see their jokes, their rivalries and their competitive games as individuals come and go.

Scene: A street in a town.
PENNY and VAL appear.

VAL   Where is the party, though?

PENNY   I don't know … it's somewhere round here. What's Willie doing? (*WILLIE enters, trailing his foot.*)

WILLIE   Orr, I've got dog-cack on me shoe!

PENNY   Oh, Willie! Wipe it off then!

WILLIE   I can't!

PENNY   Well, take your shoe off, then!

(*WILLIE removes his shoe. They all look at it and go 'Yeeeurgh!' Willie cannot resist having a close-up sniff.*)

WILLIE   Poooh! It stinks! Smell it!

PENNY   I can already smell it from here!

WILLIE   (*Thrusting the shoe at PENNY*) Smell it close! Go on!

PENNY   Nooo-o! Take it away!

WILLIE   I dare you to smell it!

PENNY   No, I'm not going to smell it!

WILLIE   Well … Touch it then! Go on! You daren't.

VAL   No! Don't! (*PENNY decides to touch it.*)

PENNY   Yeeurgh! Err, it's all yacky and squidgy!

VAL   Orr, Penny! Err … it's horrible!

PENNY   What shall I do with it?

WILLIE   Get Valerie to lick it off!!

VAL   No! Take it away!

PENNY   Orr, alright, I'll wipe it on this lamp-post.

WILLIE   Yeeach! I hate ten-foots – they're horrible!

PENNY   No, they're not … they're good – I wish we had one!

WILLIE   I don't! They're dirty and smelly and common …

(*MARTIN appears suddenly through his gate and crosses straight to Willie.*)

MARTIN I'm gonna smack you!

WILLIE   (*Leaping back in alarm*) What for?

PENNY (*Standing in front of Willie*) No, you're not!

MARTIN Yeah, I am. I'm gonna smack you!

WILLIE   No you're not, then … 'cos I'll rub dog-cacca up your nose!

PENNY   Yeah! Go on, Willie!

(*WILLIE thrusts the shoe at MARTIN'S face. MARTIN backs off, squirming. WILLIE presses forward the attack.*)

WILLIE (*Turning back*) He's running away, Penny! He's running.

(*MARTIN advances.*)

WILLIE   He's coming back. Penny! He's coming back!!

MARTIN I'm gonna really smack you for that now!

(*WILLIE retreats and PENNY steps in front to protect him.*)

PENNY   Don't you dare touch my Willie!

(*MARTIN can't prevent himself from bursting out laughing at this.*)

MARTIN You 'aven't got a willie!

PENNY   Don't be rude, you! That's my Willie!

WILLIE   Yeah, and that's my Penny … and that's my Valerie – well, she's not mine, 'cos she's not my sister … but she's somebody's Valerie.

MARTIN I'm still gonna smack you!

WILLIE   Why?

MARTIN 'Cos you've been shoving my brother about!

WILLIE   No I haven't! I don't even know your brother!

PENNY   No, we don't … and anyway, Willie doesn't hit anybody, do you?

WILLIE   No! We only just got here as well … and I trod in this dog-cacca … I bet you did it!

PENNY   Yeah! You're a dog!

WILLIE   Yeah, you are! Woof, woof, woof.

(*PENNY and VAL join in the barking and teasing. Meanwhile, CHARLIE opens her gate and comes out.*)

MARTIN   No I'm not a dog!

WILLIE   Yes you are – you look like one!

CHARLIE (*Very affectionately*) Hiya Martin!

PENNY   Who's that!

WILLIE   That's your girlfriend, isn't it?

CHARLIE Yes!

MARTIN   No!

PENNY   Yes she is, then – she said so!

WILLIE   Yaargh! He's got a girlfriend!

John Lee

TEXT LEVEL WORK

Comprehension

A 1 Where are Val and Penny going when they meet Willie?

2 Why does Martin want to hit Willie?

3 Why does Martin deny that he has got a girlfriend?

4 Why does Willie hate '*ten-foots*'?

5 Why does Penny defend Willie from Martin?

B 1 Is Martin really Charlie's boyfriend?

2 Has Willie really been shoving Martin's brother about?

3 Why does Penny accuse Martin of being a dog?

4 What evidence is there in the scene to suggest that Martin really is Charlie's boyfriend?

5 What ages do you think the characters are?

C 1 In what ways does the scene capture the mischievous humour of children?

2 Is the aggression and threatening behaviour of the characters in the scene typical of children's relationships?

WORD LEVEL WORK

Vocabulary

Dictionary work

In this playscript, the author has used a good deal of children's *Slang* and street talk, eg

'Orright, mate?'

This is informal language and it is more common in speech than in writing.

Often, written English is more formal, avoiding slang. This more formal style of language is sometimes called *Standard English*, eg

'Good morning, my friend.'

Copy the table below. Use a dictionary and the context of the play scene to translate the Slang into Standard English.

Slang	Standard English
Orr, I've got dog-cack on me shoe!	
They all look at it and go 'Yeeeurgh!'	
Poooh! It stinks! Smell it!	
Yeeurgh! Err, it's all yacky and squidgy!	
Orr, Penny! Err … it's horrible!	
Orr, alright, I'll wipe it on this lamp-post,	
Yeeach! I hate ten-foots – they're horrible!	
Yeah, I am. I'm gonna smack you!	
No you're not, then … 'cos I'll rub dog-cacca up your nose!	
Woof, woof, woof!	
Hiya Martin!	
Yaargh! He's got a girlfriend!	

Spelling

Contractions and 'not' words

> A *contraction* is used instead of two words, eg
>
> 'What's Willie doing?'
>
> 'What's' is a contraction of 'What is'.
> Contractions are made by leaving out some letters and putting an apostrophe (') in their place, eg
>
> you have = you've
>
> In 'you've' the apostrophe replaces the letters 'ha' of 'have'.
>
> Some common contractions involve 'not', eg
>
> 'Willie wouldn't behave like that if his mum was there.'
>
> 'Wouldn't' is a contraction of 'would not'.

Write these contractions as two words.

1 it's   4 I'm   7 I'll   10 he's
2 I've   5 daren't   8 they're   11 'aven't
3 can't   6 don't   9 you're   12 that's

SENTENCE LEVEL WORK

Grammar and punctuation

Punctuating a playscript

> In *Kidsplay*, the writer tries to make the characters sound natural. He has tried to convey a sense of the natural rhythms of children's speech and conversation. He has used *punctuation* to suggest the natural tones, pauses and rhythms of talk in the dialogue.

An *exclamation mark* (!) is used to give emphasis or to stress a word or phrase, eg

> MICHAEL   No! Gerrout!

Dots (.) are often used to show a dramatic pause, eg

> VAL   Orr, Penny! Err ... it's horrible!

Dashes (–) are often used to show that there should be emphasis on what comes next. A dash is sometimes followed by an exclamation mark to reinforce the emphasis, eg

> JENNY   Yes she has – there!

A Copy and complete the table to show how the author has used punctuation in the extract to represent natural speech.

Punctuation	Number of times used	Reason for use
!!! exclamation marks		
... repeated dots		
– – – dashes		

B Copy the extract below and punctuate it. Look for:

- sentence punctuation
- contractions
- punctuation for emphasis, pauses etc.

JENNY	Oorrrrgh Ive sat in something wet
CHARLIE	Itll be a puggle
JENNY	Orr me bums wet Charlotte She sticks it in Charlies direction
CHARLIE	Gerraway Dont
JENNY	Robyn me bums all wet look She points it at Robyn
ROBYN	Giyup I dont want to see it

TEXT LEVEL WORK

Writing

Dramatic dialogue

Although we all know how to talk, it is not easy to write *dramatic dialogue*. It is hard to capture a sense of the rhythms of speech, the tones of voice and how the conversations flow – in other words, to make the characters sound natural.

Playwrights have to decide what kind of people their characters are. They have to imagine how the characters would react and imagine them speaking.

Language features
Dramatic dialogue
A playwright has to think about the characters and decide:

- how they would speak
- if they have an accent
- if they speak Slang or Standard English
- what kind of vocabulary do they use
- how they would speak in the particular situation they are in.

Punctuation
Once the playwright has decided what the characters are like and how they would speak, he has to use punctuation to make it sound natural.

Remember. The punctuation marks create pauses

- for characters to think
- to gain control of their feelings
- to build up emotions.

Use exclamation marks (!) to show emphasis or stress on a particular word or phrase.
Use dots (.) to create dramatic pauses.
Use dashes (–) to show that what follows is important or should be stressed.

Writing assignment
1 Imagine a setting. It could be anywhere: a room in a house, an alley in a city, a clearing in a wood or a capsule in a space vehicle.

2 Imagine two characters who are very different. The list of character types below may help you to choose:
- aggressive, emotional, bully
- calm, reasonable, mature
- timid, shy, cries easily
- likeable, cheeky, everybody's friend
- sensible, popular, responsible
- independent, a bit of a 'tomboy'
- sweet and pretty, dominated by others
- 'loner', strong silent type.

3 Imagine a situation in which one of the characters wants or needs something badly but there is a problem getting it!

Write the dialogue for the two characters in the scene. Remember to use the appropriate punctuation to show the characters' feelings through their tone of voice, by using pauses and exclamations.

Personal choice
Choose one of the following assignments.
1 Tell the story of an event from your childhood, in which bullying or violence occurred.
2 Write a narrative poem to tell the story of your first serious argument or fight.

Hey Blousey

The action takes place in New York, in 1929. It is the era of gangsters and 'prohibition', when the buying and selling of alcohol in public places was banned. The gangsters fought for control of the illegal trade in alcohol, sold in their secret clubs known as 'speakeasies'. Our scene concentrates on Blousey, who has always wanted to be a famous singer, dancer and actress. She works in a 'speakeasy', but hopes to become a Hollywood starlet. Bugsy Malone is of Irish-Italian background, and is not completely honest but not completely crooked either. He is a 'smooth operator' who 'wheels and deals' on the edges of the gangster world.

The lights come up on BUGSY in the phone booth at the side of the stage.

BLOUSEY   Hello.

BUGSY   Hey Blousey, it's Bugsy.

BLOUSEY   Where are you?

BUGSY   Oh around. Listen. I can't talk to you now but I've just made two hundred bucks.

BLOUSEY   You mean you printed it yourself?

BUGSY   No I earned it, swear to God. (*Crosses himself*)

BLOUSEY   Doing what?

BUGSY   Oh this and that.

BLOUSEY   Who for?

BUGSY   Fat Sam.

BLOUSEY   Fat Sam gave you 200 dollars?

BUGSY   And the loan of his sedan for the afternoon.

BLOUSEY   I don't believe you. You're putting me on.

BUGSY   Look, if you get yourself outside the Grand Slam in ten minutes, look for the snazzy sedan with the good lookin' driver and you'll find he has a very close resemblance to yours truly ... O.K. ... ?

BLOUSEY   O.K. But you'd better not be putting me on, Buster.

BUGSY   Cross my heart it's on the level. So long.

(*The light goes down on BUGSY and BLOUSEY puts on her hat and coat and exits during the next scene.*)

BANGLES   Date Blousey?

BLOUSEY   Sort of.

BANGLES   I'm giving up guys, they're nothin' but trouble, believe me. From now on I'm lookin' for husbands. And I ain't getting too attached. I'm gonna change 'em regular like a library book. Hey! Don't you think I look cute? What do you think of the dress Tillie?

TILLIE   I don't know, it's ...

BANGLES   Come on Dotty, what do you think?

DOTTY   Er, well, I don't know Bangles, maybe the colour's wrong.

BANGLES   What are you talking about? Purple's my colour. I always wear purple.

LORETTA   (*Sarcastically*) Yeah, it matches the veins in your legs.

DOTTY   Maybe it's the length.

BANGLES   It's the latest length. I read it in a magazine.

VELMA   Maybe it's the frills, they stick out too much.

LORETTA   They match her ears.

BANGLES   (*Angry*) Do you think it'll look any better on you?

LORETTA   It'll look better on a horse.

BANGLES   You're just jealous. Can I help it if my looks are ahead of my time?

ALL   They're what?

BANGLES   (*Sexily*) Full of personality ... character ... kinda *earthy* ...

TALLULAH   Yeah, like a bucket of mud.

(*The girls all laugh as BANGLES storms out. Lights down. Musical reprise of 'I'm Feeling Fine'. Lights up on side of stage where BLOUSEY is sitting on a swing. BUGSY enters with two hot dogs.*)

BUGSY   Mustard with onions, ketchup without.

BLOUSEY   Ketchup without. Do you really have 200 dollars?

BUGSY   Nope.

BLOUSEY   Oh yeah, you lied.

BUGSY   No, I've got 198 dollars and ten cents – I just bought two hot dogs.

BLOUSEY   You didn't do anything crooked, did you?

BUGSY   Of course not. I got it for driving and for helping Mr Sam out of a little predicament. Oh, I nearly forgot.

(*He hands a parcel to her. A big shoe-box tied with a ribbon.*)

BLOUSEY   What's this, a fingerbowl?

BUGSY   No, a present wisie!

BLOUSEY   For me?

BUGSY (*he looks around him*) Well I didn't buy it for the audience ...

BLOUSEY   Oh Bugsy, it's wonderful. Fantastic. What is it?

(*She looks through the wrong end of an old photo viewer.*)

BUGSY   A viewer, dummy.

(*He turns it round the correct way.*) Look, you turn the handle. All the Hollywood stars.

BLOUSEY   Oh, if only I could get to Hollywood.

BUGSY   You can.

BLOUSEY   Oh sure, I've heard that one, wise guy ... in the front row of the Roxy on East 38th Street.

BUGSY   No, *really* get to Hollywood. (*She beckons back with her thumb.*) You want me to leave?

BLOUSEY   No, push me, dummy, and keep talking.

BUGSY   I've got 198 dollars and 10 cents left, right? What does that buy?

BLOUSEY   Er ... (*Counting on her fingers*) 440 hot dogs.

BUGSY   No, two tickets, stupid.

BLOUSEY   Two tickets?

BUGSY   On the Super Chief.

BLOUSEY   Super Chief?

BUGSY   The train, dummy! To Hollywood. Think about it.

(*There is silence. BUGSY moves away and starts to clean his fingers with a napkin.*)

BLOUSEY (*Swinging and singing to herself*)

  I'm feeling fine.
  Filled with emotions
  Stronger than wine
  They give me the notion
  That this strange new feeling
  Is something that you're feeling too.
  ... too ... too ...

Two tickets?

BUGSY (*over his shoulder*) Yeah, two tickets.

BLOUSEY (*singing quietly*)

  Matter of fact,
  I'm forced to admit it,
  I'm caught in the act,
  and maybe we've hit it,
  If this strange new feeling
  is something that you're feeling too
  ... oo ... oo ...

BUGSY   So what's the answer?

BLOUSEY   Did you honestly think it'd be anything but yes? Oh Bugsy ... (*she embraces him*) Hollywood!

Alan Parker

TEXT LEVEL WORK

Comprehension

A 1 How does Blousey react when Bugsy tells her, '*I've just made two hundred bucks.*'?

2 What has Fat Sam given to Bugsy?

3 What is Bangles' attitude to husbands?

4 What present does Bugsy give to Blousey?

5 What does Bugsy suggest to Blousey that they can do with the money he has earned?

B 1 In what ways do the language and the setting suggest that the play is based in America?

2 What evidence is there that Bangles is not particularly well liked?

3 How does the audience know that Blousey finds it hard to trust Bugsy?

4 What impression does the audience get of Fat Sam from Blousey and Bugsy in this scene?

5 What do we learn about Blousey's feelings from the song, 'I'm Feeling Fine'?

C 1 How far do you think that this scene shows the awkwardness of young people's relationships?

2 In what ways does this scene describe the romantic dreams of young people?

WORD LEVEL WORK

Vocabulary

Dictionary work

Use a dictionary and the context of the scene to explain the meanings of the following words.

1 sedan	4 dollars	7 snazzy	10 napkin
2 resemblance	5 notion	8 ketchup	11 fingerbowl
3 predicament	6 bucks	9 crooked	12 cents

Spelling

Apostrophes of possession (singular)

> Remember. Apostrophes (') are used in contractions to replace letters that have been left out. For example:
>
> BLOUSEY   You did**n't** do anything crooked, did you?
>
> The apostrophe shows where 'o' has been left out.
>
> Apostrophes are also used to show that someone or something owns, or possesses, an object, eg
>
> Bugsy**'s** hot-dog = the hot-dog belonging to Bugsy
>
> The **'s** makes Bugsy into a *possessive noun*.

A Write each phrase in a shorter way, using a possessive noun.
The first one has been done for you.

The money belonging to Bugsy   =   Bugsy's money

1 the dress belonging to Bangles   2 the sedan belonging to Fat Sam

3 the present belonging to Blousey   4 the tickets belonging to Bugsy

5 the ambition of Blousey

B Copy each phrase and write down whether the word in bold type is a contraction or a possessive noun. The first one has been done for you.

Blousey's dream   =   possessive noun

1 **Bugsy's** smart   2 Fat **Sam's** predicament

3 **Tillie's** uncertain   4 **Loretta's** sarcasm

5 **Blousey's** romantic

SENTENCE LEVEL WORK

Grammar and punctuation

Standard English

When we write, we usually use English as carefully and correctly as possible. Often, the language is more formal in writing than in speaking. This is called *Standard English*. When we speak, we don't use English quite so carefully or correctly.

In playscripts, although the language has to appear as if it is the language of everyday speech, it is carefully designed to appear natural. In the extract above, the playwright has used language to:

- imitate the gangster films of the 1940s and 1950s
- suggest an American setting
- convey an impression of fast-thinking, street-wise, show-business characters.

Copy the phrases and sentences below, changing them into Standard English.

1 You're putting me on.
2 You get yourself outside the Grand Slam in ten minutes.
3 He has a very close resemblance to yours truly.
4 Cross my heart it's on the level.
5 So long.
6 And I ain't getting too attached.
7 Purple's my colour.
8 It's the latest length.
9 Can I help it if my looks are ahead of my time?
10 You didn't do anything crooked, did you?
11 No, a present wisie!
12 A viewer, dummy.

TEXT LEVEL WORK

Writing

Storyboarding a play scene

One way to communicate the action taking place in a playscript is to prepare a *storyboard*. A storyboard presents the action as a series of frames, like a comic book or cartoon.

A storyboard contains a number of frames that can be used to guide film-makers in preparing to 'shoot' a film. Each frame in the storyboard will give information to the film-makers.

The information conveyed by a storyboard includes:

- the type of camera shot
- the angle of the camera

- the movement and direction of the camera
- the timing of the camera shot
- the dialogue spoken
- special effects, eg visual or sound.

Below is an example of one frame from a storyboard. It contains the information needed to guide a cameraman. Use it to help you to complete the writing assignment below.

High camera angle   Medium camera shot

Zoom in slowly for 5 seconds

Cut right to next camera shot →

Special effects = pool of blood slowly seeping from under the body
Dialogue = Nobody squeals on Fat Sam!

Writing assignment

Make a storyboard for one of the following:

- Bugsy's and Blousey's telephone conversation
- Blousey's scene with Bangles and the other girls
- Blousey's meeting with Bugsy.

Personal choice

Choose one of the following assignments.

1 Write the opening sequence for a gangster story. Try to develop an opening that has something unusual about it, eg a shocking discovery or a story with a different structure.

2 Write a climax for a gangster story in which two deadly rivals finally meet and only one will survive.

Text © Wendy Wren and Geoff Reilly 2002

Original illustrations © Nelson Thornes Ltd 2002

The right of Wendy Wren and Geoff Reilly to be identified as authors of this work has been asserted by them in accordance with the Copyright, Designs and Patents Act 1988.

All rights reserved. No part of this publication may be reproduced or transmitted in any form or by any means, electronic or mechanical, including photocopy, recording or any information storage and retrieval system, without permission in writing from the publisher or under licence from the Copyright Licensing Agency Limited, of 90 Tottenham Court Road, London W1T 4LP.

Any person who commits any unauthorised act in relation to this publication may be liable to criminal prosecution and civil claims for damages.

Published in 2002 by:
Nelson Thornes Ltd
Delta Place
27 Bath Road
CHELTENHAM
GL53 7TH
United Kingdom

02 03 04 05 06 / 10 9 8 7 6 5 4 3 2

A catalogue record for this book is available from the British Library

ISBN 0-7487-6541-7

Illustration by Pat Williams
Designed by Viners Wood Associates

Printed and bound in Italy by Canale

Acknowledgements
The authors and publishers are grateful to the following for permission to reproduce copyright material and photographs for this book:

Jonathan Clowes Ltd. on behalf of Pluriform Publishing Company BV for material from Len Deighton, Declarations of War, Granada Publishing (1971) pp.105-6, 108-9. Copyright © 1971 Len Deighton, © 2000 Pluriform Publishing Company BV; Curtis Brown on behalf of The Chichester Partnership for material from Daphne du Maurier, Rebecca, Gollancz (1938) pp.7-9. Copyright © Daphne du Maurier 1938; and on behalf of Eric Robinson for John Clare, 'The Badger', edited by Eric Robinson. Copyright © Eric Robinson; Faber and Faber Ltd for material from William Golding, Lord of The Flies (1954) pp.44-6; HarperCollins Publishers, Australia, for Ernest G Moll, 'Foxes Among the Lambs' from Poems 1940-1955 by Ernest G Moll; HarperCollins Publishers Ltd for material from Alice Borchardt, The Silver Wolf, Voyager (1999) pp.7-9; David Higham Associates on behalf of the author for Charles Causley, 'My Mother Saw a Dancing Bear' from Figgie Hobbin, Macmillan (1970); John Lee for material from Kidsplay by John Lee, Act Now Plays, Cambridge University Press (1989) pp.32-5; National Film Trustee Company Ltd for material from Alan Parker, Bugsy Malone (1984); Pavilion Books, a division of Chrysalis Books Plc for material from Michael Foreman, War Game, (1993) pp.71-93. Copyright © Michael Foreman 1993; Pearson Education Ltd for material from Michael Church and Elizabeth Tadman, 'Animal Rights' from Plays for Today, Longman (1987) pp.2-6. Copyright © Michael Church and Elizabeth Tadman 1987; Penguin UK for Robert Cormier, The Chocolate War, Gollancz (1975) pp.7-9. Copyright © Robert Cormier 1975; The Random House Group Ltd for material from Franz Kafka, Metamorphosis, Martin Secker & Warburg (1999) pp.9-12; Ivan Southall & Co Pty Ltd for material from Ash Road by Ivan Southall, Angus & Robertson (1966) pp.21-3; A P Watt Ltd on behalf of the Literary Executors of the Estate of the author for material from H G Wells, The War of the Worlds (1898).

Corel (NT), p.10; Corel (NT), p. 16; Digital Vision (NT) p. 22; Corel (NT) p. 52; Viners Wood Associates, page 58; Corel (NT), p. 70; Corel (NT), Corel (NT), p. 82; Corel (NT) p. 88; Sylvia Cordaiy Photo Library Ltd, p. 100; Corel (NT), p. 106.

Every effort has been made to trace the copyright holders but if any have been inadvertently overlooked the publishers will be pleased to make the necessary arrangement at the first opportunity.